HINDOO TALES

HINDOO TALES

OR, THE ADVENTURES OF TEN PRINCES

FREELY TRANSLATED FROM THE SANSCRIT OF
THE DASAKUMARACHARITAM

P. W. JACOB

GYAN

Published by

Gyan Publishing House
5, Ansari Road
Daryaganj, New Delhi-110002
Phone: 011-47034999, 9811692060
E-mail: books@gyanbooks.com

Distribution Network
gyanbooks.com
India, USA, Canada, UK, Australia, France

ISBN: 978-81-212-8957-3 (PB)
First Published, 1873

2nd Impression 2023

Printed at: Gyan Press, Delhi.

HINDOO TALES

AUTHOR: P. W. JACOB

HINDOO TALES

HINDOO TALES

OR, THE ADVENTURES OF TEN PRINCES

FREELY TRANSLATED FROM THE SANSCRIT OF THE DASAKUMARACHARITAM

BY

P. W. JACOB

STRAHAN & CO.
56 LUDGATE HILL, LONDON
1873

TRANSLATOR'S PREFACE.

THE Sanscrit work entitled "Dasakumara-charitam, or the Adventures of Ten Princes," though printed more than twenty-five years ago, has not, as far as I can ascertain, been translated into any European language. Many parts of it are written in such a turgid "Oriental" style, that a close translation would be quite unsuitable to the English reader. Such passages have therefore been much condensed; others, which are hardly decent—or, as in the speech of the parasite in the last story, tedious and uninteresting, have been omitted; but in general the original has been pretty closely adhered to, and nothing has been added to it.

The exact date of the composition of the "Dasakumaracharitam" is not known. It is supposed to have been written about the end of the eleventh century, and was left unfinished by the author; but as the story of the last narrator is almost finished, not much could have been wanting to complete the work, and the reader may easily imagine what the conclusion would have been.

Some of the incidents correspond with those of the "Arabian Nights," but the stories on the whole are quite different from anything found there, and give a lively picture of Hindoo manners and morals. Unscrupulous deception, ready invention, extreme credulity and superstition, and disregard of human life, are strongly illustrated.

The belief in the power of penance, which was supposed to confer on the person practising it not merely personal sanctity, but even great supernatural powers, was very generally entertained among the Hindoos, and is often alluded to here; as is also transmigration, or the birth of the soul after death in a new body, human or brute. Sufferings or misfortunes are attributed to sins committed in a former existence, and in more than one story two persons are supposed to recollect having many years before lived together as husband and wife.

Much use also is made of the agency of supernatural beings; for besides numerous gods, the Hindoos believe, or at least believed, in the existence of innumerable beings, in some degree immortal, but liable to be killed even by men, swarming in the air, generally invisible, but sometimes assuming a human or a more terrible form; occasionally beneficent, but more commonly injurious to human beings.

At the time when the original work was written, India appears to have been divided into a large number of small kingdoms or principalities, the rulers of which are here termed "Rāja," a word almost adopted into our language, but which I have rendered by the equivalent and more familiar term "King."

The numerous uncouth names, which cannot well be shortened or translated, will, it is feared, cause some annoyance to the reader. As many as possible have been omitted, and of those which occur a list is given in the Appendix, together with a few terms which seemed to require explanation. This will save the reader the trouble of referring, when a name recurs, to the place where it is first mentioned in order to find out to whom it belongs.

The Appendix also contains a few pages of a very close literal translation, which will enable the reader to form some idea of the nature and style of the original, and to see how far it has been departed from in the preceding pages.

P. W. J.

GUILDFORD, *December*, 1872.

PRONUNCIATION OF PROPER NAMES.

The vowel *ā*, is always to be pronounced as in father.

" *a*, as in America, or as u in dull, i in bird, &c.

" *e*, always as a in cake.

" *í*, as e in cede, or ee in reed.

" *i*, as in pin.

" *ū*, as in flute.

" *u*, as in bull.

Pati is therefore pronounced putty, &c.

CONTENTS.

THERE was formerly, in the most fertile part of India, a city called Pushpapuri, the capital of Magadha, magnificent as a mine of jewels, abounding in every kind of wealth, surpassing all other cities in splendour and prosperity.

The sovereign of this city and country was Rājahansa, whose armies were formidable with countless elephants and horses, whose glory was unsullied as the moon in a cloudless sky, or the plumage of the swan, and whose fame was sung even by celestial minstrels. Though a terror to his enemies, he was beloved by all his subjects, and especially by the learned and pious brahmans, who were continually employed in prayers and sacrifices to the gods, for the welfare of the king and his people.

The queen Vasumati was worthy of such a husband. She was of high birth and of a sweet temper, and so great was her beauty that it seemed as if the god of love had formed her for his own special delight, by uniting in her single person everything that is most beautiful in the world.

Among the king's counsellors were three appointed to the highest offices of state, men of great probity and intelligence, who had been long in his father's service and enjoyed his entire confidence. Their names were, Dharmapāla, Padmodbhava, and Sitavarma.

The first of these had three sons, Sumantra,

Sumittra, and Kāmapāla; the second, two, Susruta and Ratnodbhava; and the last had also two, Sumati and Satyavarma.

Of these sons the last-mentioned renounced worldly cares and employments, devoted himself to religious meditation, and leaving home as a pilgrim, travelled into many countries in order to visit the holy places which they contained.

Kāmapāla was of an opposite character; he thought only of present pleasure, frequented the company of gamblers and harlots, and roamed about the world seeking amusement and dissipation.

Ratnodbhava became a merchant, and in the way of traffic made many long journeys by land and sea. The other sons, after their fathers' death, succeeded to their offices, according to the custom of the country.

When Rājahansa had reigned some years, war broke out between him and the king of the adjoining country of Mālwa, the haughty and ambitious Mānasāra, whom he marched to encounter with a numerous army, making the earth tremble with the tread of his elephants, and disturbing even the dwellers in the sky with the clang of kettledrums louder than the roar of the stormy ocean.

Both armies were animated by equal rage, and terrible was the battle; the ground where they met was first turned to dust by the wheels of the chariots and the trampling of men and beasts, and then into mud through the streams of blood which flowed from the slain and wounded.

At last Rājahansa was victorious, the enemy was completely defeated, their king taken prisoner, and all Mālwa lay open to the conqueror. He, however, having no wish to enlarge his dominions, released his prisoner on very easy terms, and returning to Pushpapuri, thought only of governing his own kingdom in peace, not expecting after such generous treatment any further trouble from his ambitious neighbour.

Though prosperous and happy in every other respect, the King of Magadha had one great cause of sorrow and anxiety—he had no son to succeed him. Therefore, at this time he made many prayers and offerings to Nārāyana the Creator of the World, who, having been thus propitiated, signified to the queen in a dream that she would bear a son; and not long afterwards her husband was gratified by the news of her pregnancy.

When the proper time arrived the king

celebrated the ceremony called Símanta* with great magnificence, and invited several of the neighbouring kings to be present on the occasion; among them was the King of Mithila, with his queen, a great friend of Vasumati — to congratulate whom she had accompanied her husband.

One day after this, when the king was sitting in council with his ministers, he was informed that a certain venerable Yati was desirous to see him. On his admission the king perceived that he was one of his secret emissaries; dismissing, therefore, the rest of the counsellors, he withdrew to a private apartment, followed by one or two of his most confidential ministers and the supposed Yati. He, bowing down to the ground, said in answer to the king's

* A religious ceremony on behalf of a woman at a certain period of pregnancy.

inquiry, "In order the better to perform your Majesty's commands, I have adopted this safe disguise, and have resided for some time in the capital of Mālwa, from whence I now bring very important news. The haughty Mānasāra, brooding over his defeat, unmindful of your generous forbearance, and only anxious to wipe off his disgrace, has been for a long time endeavouring to propitiate with very severe penance the mighty Siva, whose temple is at Mahākāla, and he has so far succeeded that the god has given him a magic club, very destructive of life and conducive to victory.

"Through this weapon, and the favour of Siva, he now thinks himself a match for you. He has for some time been strengthening his army, and will probably very soon invade this country. Your Majesty having received this information, will decide what ought to be done."

On hearing this report the ministers consulted together and said to the king, "This enemy is coming against us favoured by the gods, and you cannot hope to resist him; we therefore advise that you should avoid fighting, and retire with your family and treasure to a strong fortress."

Although they urged this advice with many reasons, it was not acceptable to the king, who determined to march at the head of his army against the invaders. When, however, the enemy had actually entered the country, the ministers succeeded in persuading their master to send away the queen and her attendants, and a part of the treasure, to a strong fortress in the forest of Vindhya, guarded by veteran soldiers.

Presently the two armies met, the battle raged furiously, and Mānasāra, eagerly seeking out his former conqueror, at last encountered his chariot. Wielding the magic club, with one blow he slew the charioteer and caused the king to fall down senseless.

The horses being freed from control, suddenly turned round, dashed off at full speed from the field, and never stopped till, utterly exhausted, they had dragged the chariot with the still insensible king very near to the fortress to which the queen had retreated.

Meanwhile, some of the fugitives from the battle, having reached the fortress, told the queen what had happened, and she, overwhelmed by grief at the death of her husband, determined not to survive him. Perceiving her purpose, the old brahmans and faithful counsellors, who had accompanied her, endeavoured to dissuade her, saying, "O glorious lady, we have no certain information of the king's death: moreover, learned astrologers have declared that the child to be born of you is destined to become a mighty sovereign, therefore do not act rashly or end so precious a life while the least hope remains."

Apparently influenced by these reasons, eloquently urged, the queen remained silent, and seemed to renounce her purpose, but at midnight, unable to sleep, and oppressed by intolerable grief, she rose up, and evading her sleeping attendants and the guards outside, went into the forest, and there, after many passionate lamentations and prayers that she might rejoin her beloved husband, she formed a rope by twisting a part of her dress, and was preparing to hang herself with it from the branch of a tree, very near to the place where the chariot was standing concealed by the thick foliage.

Just then the king, revived by the cool night wind, recovered consciousness, and hearing his wife's voice, softly called her by name. She, hardly believing her senses for joy, cried out loudly for help, and soon brought to her assistance some of the attendants, who carried him gently into the fort, where his wounds were dressed and found not to be dangerous.

After a short time, more of those who had escaped joined the king; and when he was sufficiently recovered, the charming Vasumati, instructed by the ministers, said to him, "All your dominions are lost except this fortress; but such is the power of fate; prosperity, like a bubble on the water, or a flash of lightning, appears and disappears in a moment. Former kings, Rāmachandra and others, at least as great as yourself, were deprived of their kingdoms, and suffered for a long time the hardships of adversity; yet, through patience and perseverance and the will of fate, they were at last restored to all their former splendour. Do you therefore imitate them, and, laying aside all anxiety, devote yourself to prayer and meditation."

To this advice the king gave ear, and went to consult a very celebrated rishi, Vāmadeva, intending, under his directions, to engage in such penance as might lead to the accomplishment of his wishes.

Having been well received by the holy man, he said to him: "O father, having heard of your great piety and wisdom, I have come hither for guidance and help in a great calamity. Mānasāra, King of Mālwa, has overcome me, and now holds the kingdom which ought to be mine. I will shrink from no penance which you shall advise, if by such means I may obtain the favour of the gods, and be restored to my former power."

Vāmadeva, well acquainted with all past, present, and future events, thus answered him: "O friend, there is no need of penance in your case; only wait patiently; a son will certainly be born to you who will crush all your enemies and restore your fortunes." Then a voice was heard in the air, saying, "This is true."

The king, fully believing the prophecy of the muni, thus miraculously confirmed, returned to the forest, resolved to await patiently the fulfilment of the promise; and shortly afterwards the queen brought forth a son possessing all good marks,* to whom his father gave the name of Rājavāhana.

About the same time also sons were born to his four ministers. They were named severally Pramati, Mitragupta, Mantragupta, and Visruta, and were brought up together with the young prince.

Some time after the birth of these children, a certain muni brought a very beautiful boy to the king, and said: "Having gone lately into the forest to collect kusa-grass† and fuel, I met a woman, evidently in great distress. When I questioned her, she wiped away her tears, and told me, with a voice broken by sobs, that she was a servant of Prahāravarma,

* The Hindoos attach much importance to certain marks on the body, such as the lines on the hands, &c.

† Kusa-grass, or kuskus, is used for strewing the floor of a sacrificial enclosure, for laying offerings on, and for other sacred uses.

King of Mithila—that he, with his family, had gone to Pushpapuri, to be present at the Símanta festival of the queen, and had stayed there some time after the departure of the other guests; that at that time the King of Mālwa, furnished with a magic weapon, had invaded the country; that in the battle which ensued, Prahāravarma had assisted his friend with the few soldiers who accompanied him, and had been taken prisoner, but had been liberated by the conqueror; that on his return he had been attacked in the forest by Bheels, and had repulsed them with difficulty. 'I and my daughter,' she continued, 'who had charge of the king's twin children, were separated from the rest in the confusion, and lost our way in the forest. There we suddenly came upon a tiger. In my fright, I stumbled and fell, and dropped the child, which I was carrying, on the carcase of a cow with which the tiger had been engaged. At that moment an arrow struck and killed the tiger. I fainted away, and when I recovered, I found myself quite alone; my daughter had disappeared, and the child, as I suppose, was carried off by the Bheels, who shot the beast. After a time I was found by a compassionate cowherd, who took care of me till my wounds were healed; and I am now wandering about in the hope of finding the boy, and of hearing some tidings of my daughter and the other child.' After giving me this account, she went on her way again, and I, distressed that the son of your majesty's friend should be in such hands, determined to set out in search of him.

"After some days I came to a small temple of Durga, where a party of Bheels were about to make the child an offering to the goddess, in the hope of obtaining success through her favour; and they were then deliberating in what manner they should kill him, whether by hanging him on the branch of a tree and cutting him to pieces with swords, or by partly burying him in the ground and shooting at him with arrows, or by worrying him with young dogs.

"Then I went up to them very humbly, and said: 'O Kirātas, I am an old brahman; having lost my way in the forest, I laid down my child whom I was carrying, while I went away for a moment to try to find an opening out of the dense thicket; when I came back he was gone. I have been searching for him ever since; have you seen him?' 'Is this your child?' said they. 'O, yes!' I exclaimed. 'Take him, then,' they replied; 'we respect a brahman.' Thus I got possession of the boy, and, blessing them for their kindness, took him away as quickly as possible, and have now brought him here, thinking he will be best under your majesty's protection."

The king, though grieved at the calamity of his friend, rejoiced that the child was saved from such a death; and giving him the name of Upahāravarma, had him brought up as his own son.

Not long after this, Rājahansa went to bathe at a holy place, and in returning, as he passed by a group of Chandālas, he observed a woman carrying a very beautiful boy. Being struck by the appearance of the child, he said: "Where did you get this beautiful boy, who is like a king's son? Surely he is not your own child! pray tell me."

She answered: "When the Bheels attacked and plundered the King of Mithila near our village, this child was picked up and brought to me by my husband, and I have taken care of him ever since."

The king being convinced that this was the other child of his friend, the King of Mithila, by fair words and gifts induced the woman to give him up, and took him to the queen, giving him the name of Apahāravarma, and begging her to bring him up with her own son.

Soon afterwards, a disciple of Vāmadeva brought a beautiful boy to the king, and said: "As I was returning from a pilgrimage to Rāmatirtha, I saw an old woman carrying this child, and asked her how she came to be wandering there. In answer to my questions, she told me her story, saying, 'I was the servant of a rich man, named Kālagupta, living in the island of Kālayavana, and I waited on his daughter Suvritta. One day a young merchant, named Ratnodbhava, son of a minister of the King of Magadha, arrived in the island, and having become acquainted with my master, he married his beautiful daughter.

"'After some time, he was desirous of visiting his family, and being unwilling to leave behind his young wife, who was then not far from childbirth, he took her with him, and me as her nurse.

"'We embarked on board a ship, and had at first a favourable voyage; but when approaching the land, we were overtaken by a storm, and a great wave broke over the ship, which went down almost immediately. I found myself in the water near my young mistress, and managed to support her till we got hold of a plank, by means of which we at last reached the shore. Whether my master was saved or not I do not know, but I fear that he perished with the rest of those on board, whom we never saw again.

"'The coast where we landed appeared to be uninhabited, and the poor lady, being unable to walk far, after much suffering of mind and body, gave birth to this child under a tree in the forest. I have just left her, in the hope of finding some village where I may obtain assistance; and by her wish I have brought the child with me, since she is incapable of taking care of it.'

"The woman had hardly finished speaking when a wild elephant, breaking through the bushes, came suddenly upon us, and she was so frightened that she let the child fall, and ran away.

"I hid myself behind a tree, and saw the elephant take up the child with his trunk, as if about to put it into its mouth. At that moment he was attacked by a lion, and let the child fall. When the two beasts had moved from the spot, I came from my hiding-place just in time to see the child taken up by a monkey, who ran up a high tree. Presently the beast let the child drop, and as it fell on a leafy branch, I took it up uninjured by the fall, or the other rough treatment which it had received.

"After searching for the woman some time in vain, I took the child to my master, the great muni Vāmadeva, and I have now brought it to you by his command."

The king, astonished at the preservation of the child under such adverse circumstances, and hoping that Ratnodbhava might have escaped from the shipwreck, sent for Susruta to take charge of his brother's child, to whom he gave the name of Pushpod-bhava.

Some days after this the queen went up to her husband with a child in her arms, and told him, when he expressed his surprise: "Last night I was suddenly awakened from sleep and saw a beautiful lady standing before me, holding this child. She said to me: 'O queen, I am a Yaksha, daughter of Manib-hadra, and wife of Kāmāpāla, the son of your husband's late minister, Dharmapāla; by command of Kuvera, I have brought this my child to you, that he may enter the service of your son, who is destined to become a mighty monarch'

"I was too much astonished to ask her any question, and she, having laid down the child near me, disappeared."

The king, greatly surprised, especially that Kāmāpāla should have married a Yaksha, sent for the child's uncle, Sumittra, and committed the boy to his care, giving him the name of Arthapāla.

Not long after this another disciple of Vāmadeva brought a very beautiful child to the king, and said: "My lord, I have lately been on a pilgrimage to several holy places, and on my way back, happening to be on the bank of the river Kāvari, I saw a woman carrying this child, and evidently in great distress. On being questioned by me, she wiped away her tears, and with difficulty told me her story, saying, 'O brahman, Satyavarma, the youngest son of Sitavarma, a minister of the King of Magadha, after travelling about a long time, visiting all holy places as a pilgrim, came to this country, and here married a Brahman's daughter, named Kālí. Having no children by her, he took as his second wife her sister Gaurí, and by her he had one son, this child.

"'Then the first wife, envious of her sister, determined to destroy the child; and having, with some false pretence, enticed me, when I was carrying the child, to the bank of the river, she pushed us in. I contrived to hold my charge with one hand, and to swim with the other till I met with an uprooted tree carried down by the rapid current. To this I clung, and after floating a long distance, was able at last to land at this place; but in getting away from the tree I disturbed a black serpent which had taken refuge there, and having been bitten by it, I now feel that I am dying.' As she spoke, the poison began to take greater effect, and she fell on the ground.

"After trying in vain the power of charms, I went to look for some herb which might serve as an antidote ; but when I returned the poor creature was dead.

"I was much perplexed at this occurrence, especially as she had not told me the name of the village from which she came, nor could I conjecture how far off it might be, so that I was unable to take the child to its father.

"Therefore, after collecting wood and burning the body, I have brought the child to you, thinking that he will be best taken care of under your protection."

The king, astonished that so many children should have been brought in such a wonderful manner, and distressed at not knowing where to find Satyavarma, gave the child the name of Somadatta, and committed him to the care of his uncle, Sumati, who received him with great affection.

These nine boys, thus wonderfully collected

together, became the associates and play-fellows of the young prince, and were educated together with him.

When they were all nearly seventeen, their education was regarded as complete, for they had not only been taught the vedas and the commentaries on them, several languages, grammar, logic, philosophy, &c., but were well acquainted with poetry, plays, and all sorts of tales and stories; were accomplished in drawing and music, skilled in games, sleight of hand and various tricks, and practised in the use of weapons. They were also bold riders and drivers of horses and elephants; and even clever thieves, able to steal without detection; so that Rājahansa was exceedingly delighted at seeing his son surrounded by a band of such brave, active, clever companions and faithful followers.

One day about this time Vāmadeva came to visit the king, by whom he was received with great respect and reverence. Seeing the prince perfect in beauty, strength, and accomplishments, and surrounded by such companions, he said to Rājahansa: "Your wish for a son has indeed been fully gratified, since you have one who is all that you could desire. It is now time for him to go out into the world and prepare himself for the career of conquest to which he is destined."

The king listened respectfully to the advice of the muni, and determined to be guided by it; having therefore given his son good advice, he sent him forth at a propitious hour, to travel about in search of adventure, accompanied by his nine friends.

After travelling for some days, they entered the forest of Vindhya, and when halting there for the night they saw a rough-looking man, having all the appearance of a Bheel, but wearing the sacred cord which is the characteristic of a brahman.

The prince, surprised at such an incongruity, asked him who he was, how he came to be living in such a wild place, and how, with all the appearance of a forester, he was wearing the brahminical cord.

The man, seeming to be aware that his questioner was a person of importance, answered respectfully, "O prince, there are in this forest certain nominal brahmans, who, having abandoned the study of the vedas, religious obligations, and family duties, are devoted to all sorts of sinful practices, and act as leaders of robber bands, associating with their followers and living as they live.

"I, Matanga by name, am the son of one

of these, and was brought up to be a robber like them. Since I have been grown up I have often assisted in plundering expeditions, when they would fall suddenly on some defenceless village, and carry away not only all the property on which they could lay their hands, but several of the richest of the inhabitants, whom they would keep prisoners till a ransom had been paid, or till, compelled by torture, they confessed where their money was concealed.

"On one of these occasions, when my companions were ill-treating a brahman, I was seized by a sudden feeling of compassion and remonstrated with them. Finding words of no avail, I stood before him, and was killed by my own men while fighting on his behalf.

"After death I went down to the regions

below, and was taken before Yama, the judge of the dead, sitting on a great throne inlaid with jewels.

"When the god saw me prostrate before him he called one of his attendants and said: 'The time for this man's death is not arrived, and moreover, he was killed in defending a brahman; therefore, after showing him the tortures of the wicked, let him return to his former body, in which he will in future lead a holy life.'

"By him I was shown some sinners tied to red-hot iron bars, some thrown into great tubs of boiling oil, some beaten with clubs, some cut to pieces with swords; after which my spirit re-entered the body, and I awoke to consciousness, lying alone, grievously wounded, in the forest.

"In this state I was found by some of my

relations, who carried me home and took care of me till my wounds were healed.

"Shortly after this I met with the brahman whom I had rescued, and he, grateful for the service which I had rendered him, read to me some religious books, and taught me the due performance of religious rites, especially the proper way of worshipping Siva.

"When he considered me sufficiently instructed, he quitted me, giving me his blessing, and receiving many thanks from me for his kindness.

"Since then I have separated myself from all my former associates, and have lived a life of penance and meditation in this forest, endeavouring to atone for my past sins, and especially seeking to propitiate the mighty deity who has the half moon for his crest; and now, having told you my history, I have something to communicate which concerns you alone, and beg you to withdraw with me to hear it in private."

The two then went aside from the rest of the party, and the stranger said, "O prince, last night, during sleep, Siva appeared to me and addressed me thus: 'Matanga, I am pleased with your devotions; they shall now have their reward. North of this place, on the bank of the river which flows through the Dandaka forest, there is a remarkable rock, glittering with crystal and marked with the footsteps of Gaurí. Go thither; in the side of the rock you will see a yawning chasm, enter it and search till you find a copper plate with letters engraved on it; follow the directions therein contained, and you will become King of Pātāla. That you may know this not to be a mere dream, a king's son will come to this place to-morrow, and he will be your companion in the journey.'

"I have in consequence anxiously awaited your coming, and now entreat you to go with me to the place pointed out in the vision."

The curiosity of the prince was much excited by Matanga's story, and he readily promised to be his companion; fearing, however, that his friends would be opposed to his purpose, he did not on his return tell them anything of what he had heard, and at midnight, when they were all fast asleep, he slipped away without disturbing them, and went to join Matanga, who was waiting for him at a place which had been agreed on, and the two walked on till they came to the rock indicated by Siva in the vision.

Meanwhile, the rest of the party, uneasy at the disappearance of the prince, sought for him all over the forest, and not finding him, determined to disperse, and continue the search in different countries; and having arranged where to meet again, took leave of each other, and set out separately in different directions.

Matanga, entirely believing the vision, and rendered still more confident by the companionship of the prince, fearlessly entered the cavern, found the copper plate and read the words engraved on it. Following the directions therein contained, they went on in darkness, groping their way through long passages, till at last they saw light before them and arrived at the subterranean country of Pātāla.

After walking some distance further, they came to a small lake, surrounded by trees, with a city in view.

Here they stopped, and Matanga begging the prince to watch and guard against interruption, collected a quantity of wood and lighted a large fire, into which he threw himself with many charms and incantations, and presently came forth with a new body full of youth, beauty, and vigour, to the great astonishment of his companion.

Hardly was this change effected, when they saw coming towards them from the city a procession, headed by a beautiful young lady splendidly dressed, and adorned with very costly jewels. Approaching Matanga, she made a low obeisance, and, without speaking, put a very precious gem into his hand. Being questioned by him, she answered, with tears in her eyes and in a soft musical voice, "O excellent brahman, I am the daughter of a chief of Asuras, and my name is Kalindí; my father, the ruler of this subterranean world, was slain by Vishnu whom he had offended, and as he had no son, I was left his heir and successor, and suffered great distress and perplexity.

"Some time ago I consulted a very holy Siddha, who had compassion on me, and told me, 'After a time, a certain mortal, having a heavenly body, will come down here from the upper world; he will become your husband, and reign prosperously with you over all Pātāla.'

"Trusting to this prophecy, I have waited impatiently, longing for your coming as a Chātaka longs for rain, and am now come, with the consent of my ministers and people, to offer you my hand and kingdom."

Matanga, delighted at such a speedy fulfilment of the promise given in the vision, gladly accepted her offer, and with the approbation of his companion, was soon afterwards married to her amid great festivity.

Rājavāhana was treated with great respect and kindness by Matanga and his bride; but after seeing all the wonders of the place, his curiosity was satisfied, and he was desirous of returning to the upper world.

At his departure, a magic jewel was given him by Kalindí, which had the power of keeping off from the possessor of it hunger, thirst, fatigue, and other discomforts; and Matanga accompanied him for a part of the way. Walking through darkness as before, the prince at last reached the mouth of the cavern and came forth into the open air.

Having missed all his companions, he was uncertain where to direct his steps, and wandered on till he came to a large park, outside a city, where a great concourse of people was assembled, and he there sat down to rest.

As he sat watching the various groups, he saw a young man enter the park, accompanied by a lady and followed by a numerous retinue, and they both got into one of the swings placed there for the amusement of the festal crowd.

Presently the eye of the new-comer rested on the prince; with signs of great joy he jumped down, exclaiming, "O what happiness! That is my lord Rājavāhana," and, running to him, bowed down to his feet, saying "Great is my good fortune in meeting you again." Rājavāhana, affected by equal pleasure, warmly embraced him, saying, "O my dear friend Somadatta, how happy I am to see you once more!"

Then they sat down together under a shady tree, and the prince inquired: "What have you been doing all this time? Where have you been? Who is this lady? And how did you get all these attendants?" Somadatta, thus questioned, began the recital of what he had done and seen.

ADVENTURES OF SOMADATTA.

MY LORD, having great anxiety on your account, I wandered about in various countries. One day, when stooping to drink from a cool, clear stream, near a forest, I saw something bright under the water, and having taken it up, found it to be a ruby of very great value.

Exhausted by fatigue and the scorching heat of the sun, I went into a small temple to rest, and saw there a brahman with a number of children, all looking wretched and half-starved. He seemed to regard me as a possible benefactor, and when questioned, readily told me his story; how his wife had died, leaving him with the care of all these children, and how, having no means of subsistence, he had wandered about in the hope of obtaining some employment; but had got nothing better than the charge of this small temple, where the offerings were not sufficient to support him and his family.

I asked him—"What is that camp which I see at some distance?"

He answered—"The Lord of Lāta, Mattakāla by name, hearing again and again of the great beauty of Vāmalochana, daughter of Víraketu, sovereign of this country, asked her in marriage, and was refused. Being determined to obtain her, he raised an army and besieged Pātali, the capital city. Víraketu finding himself unable to resist the enemy, purchased peace by giving up his daughter, and Mattakāla, thinking that the marriage can be celebrated with greater magnificence in his own country, has deferred it till his return. He is now on his way home with a small part of his army, the rest having been dismissed; and he is staying at present near this forest to enjoy the pleasures of the chase. The princess is not with her intended husband, but under the care of Mānapāla, one of her father's officers, who is said to be very indignant at the surrender of the lady; you may see his camp at no great distance from the other."

While thanking the poor man for his information, a thought came into my mind—here is a very poor and deserving man, I will give him the jewel which I have found; and I did so.

He received the gift with profuse thanks, and set out immediately to try to dispose of it; while I lay down there to sleep.

After a time I was awakened by a great clamour, and saw the brahman coming towards me with his hands tied behind him, driven along, with blows of a whip and much abuse, by a party of soldiers.

On seeing me, he called out, "There is the thief; that is the man who gave me the jewel."

Upon this the soldiers let him go, and, seizing me, refused to listen to my remonstrances, or to my account of the manner in which I had found the ruby. They dragged me along with them, and having put fetters on my feet, thrust me into a dungeon, saying, "There are your companions," pointing at the same time to some other prisoners confined in that place.

When I recovered my senses—for I was half stunned by the violence with which I had been pushed in—I said to my fellow-prisoners, "Who are you, and what did the soldiers mean by calling you my companions? for you are quite strangers to me."

Those prisoners then told me the story of the King of Lāta, which I had already heard from the brahman, and further said, "We were sent by Mānapāla to assassinate that king, and broke into the place where we supposed him to be. Not finding him, we were unwilling to come away empty-handed; we therefore carried off everything of value within our reach and made our escape to the forest. The next morning there was an active pursuit, our hiding-place was discovered, we were all captured, and the stolen property taken from us, with the exception of one ruby of great value, which had disappeared. The king is exceedingly angry that this cannot be found; our assertion that we have lost it is disbelieved, and we are threatened with torture to-morrow, unless we say where it is hidden."

Having heard the robbers' story, I was convinced that the ruby in question was the one which I had found and given to the brahman, and I now understood why these men were supposed to be my accomplices.

I told them who I was, how I had found the jewel, and had been unjustly arrested on account of it, and exhorted them to take courage and join me in an attempt to escape that night. To this they agreed, and at midnight we managed to overpower the jailors and knock off our fetters; and having armed ourselves with weapons which we found in the prison, we cut our way through the guards, and reached Mānapāla's camp in safety.

The next day, men sent by the King of Lāta came to Mānapāla, and said—"Some robbers, who were caught after breaking into the king's dwelling, have made their escape, and are known to have come here; give them up immediately, or it will be the worse for you."

Mānapāla, who only wanted an excuse for a quarrel, having heard this insulting message, his eyes red with anger, answered,—"Who is the King of Lāta, that I should bow down to him? What have I to do with that low fellow? Begone!"

When the men returned to their master and told him the reception they had met with, he was in a furious rage, and, disregarding the smallness of the force which was with him, marched out at once to attack Mānapāla, who was quite prepared to meet him.

When I entered the camp, after my escape, Mānapāla, who received from his servants an exaggerated account of my coolness, dexterity, and courage, had treated me with great honour, and now I offered my services in the approaching fight. They were gladly accepted, and I was furnished with an excellent chariot and horses guided by a skilful charioteer, a strong coat of mail, a bow and two quivers full of arrows, as well as with other weapons.

Thus equipped, I went forth to meet the enemy, and seeking out the leader, soon found myself near him. First confusing him with arrows poured upon him in rapid succession, I brought my chariot close to his, and suddenly springing into it, cut off his head at a blow.

Seeing the king fall, his soldiers were

discouraged, and fled; the camp was taken, much booty gained, and the princess led back to her father. He having received an account of the victory, and of my share in it, through a messenger sent from Mānapāla, came forth to meet us when we entered the city, and received me with great honour. After a time, as I continued daily to increase in favour with him, he bestowed on me the hand of his daughter, and declared me his successor.

Being thus arrived at the height of prosperity and happiness, I had but one cause of sorrow—my absence from you. I am on my way to Mahākāla, to worship Siva there. I have stopped at this place, hoping, at a festival so much frequented, I might at least hear some tidings of you, and now the god has favoured his worshipper, and through this happy meeting all my wishes are fulfilled.

Rājavāhana, who delighted in valour, having heard Somadatta's story, while expressing his sorrow for his undeserved imprisonment, congratulated him on the happy result of it, and told him his own adventures.

He had scarcely finished the relation of them when a third person came up, and the prince, warmly greeting him, exclaimed, "O, Somadatta, here is Pushpodbhava." Then there were mutual embracings and rejoicings, after which they all three sat down again, and Rājavāhana said: "Somadatta has told me his adventures, but I know nothing of the rest of my friends. What did you do when you missed me that morning in the forest?" Then Pushbodbhava respectfully spoke as follows:—

ADVENTURES OF PUSHBODBHAVA.

MY LORD, your friends being convinced that you had gone on some expedition with the brahman, and knowing nothing of the direction which you had taken, were greatly perplexed. At last we agreed to separate, each going a different way, and I, like the rest, set out by myself. One day, being unable to bear the heat of the noonday sun, I sat down in the shade of a tree at the bottom of a mountain. Happening to look up, I saw a man falling from the rock above, and he came to the ground very near me.

On going up to him, I found that he was still alive, and having revived him by throwing cold water over him, and by other means, I found that he had no bone broken, and did not appear to have received any serious injury.

When he was sufficiently recovered, I asked him who he was and how he came to fall from the precipice. With tears in his eyes, and a feeble voice, he said: "My name is Ratnodbhava; I am the son of a minister of the King of Magadha; travelling about as a merchant, I came, many years ago, to the island of Kālayavana. There I married a merchant's daughter, and going with her by sea to visit my relations, was overtaken by a violent storm, during which the ship sank, and I was the only person saved.

"After reaching the shore, I wandered about for some time in a strange country, and, unable to bear my misery, was about to put an end to my life, when I was stopped by a Siddha, who assured me that after sixteen years I should find my wife. Trusting to this promise, I have endured life through all these years; but the appointed time having passed without any sign of the fulfilment of the prophecy, I could hold out no longer, and threw myself from the top of this precipice."

At that moment the voice of a woman in distress was heard not far off, and saying to him whom I recognised as my father, "Take courage, I have good news for you; only wait a moment," I ran off in the direction of the place whence the voice had proceeded, and soon came in sight of a large fire and two women near it, the one trying to throw herself into the flames, the other struggling to prevent her. Going to the help of the latter, I soon got the lady away, and brought her and her companion to the place where my father was lying. I then said to the old woman, "Pray tell me what all this means? How came you to be in such a place, and why did the lady wish to destroy herself?"

With a voice broken by sobs, she answered me: "This lady, whose name is Suvritta, is the daughter of a merchant in the island of Kālayavana, and the wife of Ratnodbhava. While crossing the sea with her husband, there was a great storm, the ship sank, and this lady and I, her nurse, were the only persons saved. A few days afterwards she gave birth to a son in the forest; but through my ill-fortune the child was lost, having been seized by a wild elephant. Afterwards we two wandered about in great misery, and she would have put an end to her life had we not met with a holy man, who comforted her with the assurance that after sixteen years she would be reunited with her husband and son. Relying on this prophecy, she consented to wait, and we have spent all these years living near his hermitage; but the sixteen years were ended some time ago, and having lost all hope, she was about to end her wretched life by throwing herself into a fire which she had made, when you so opportunely came to my assistance."

Hearing this story, my father was unable to speak from astonishment. I made him known to my mother, and myself to both of them, to their very great joy; and my mother seemed as if she would never weary of kissing and embracing me.

After a time, when we were all more composed, my father began to inquire about the king and his own relations, for during all these years he had heard nothing of them. I told him everything—how the king had been defeated, and had been living in the forest; your birth, and the wonderful preservation of myself and my companions; how we had all set out together; how we had lost you, and how I was now searching for you.

As soon as my father was able to walk, I placed him and my mother under the care of a certain muni, not very far off, and set out again on my travels. Just at this time I had heard that under the ruins of an ancient city, overgrown by trees, a great treasure was supposed to be concealed; and as I possessed a magic ointment which, when applied to the eyes, enabled me to see through the ground,

I determined to try to dig it up. I therefore got together some strong young men with the promise of good pay, went to the place, and succeeded in finding a large quantity of gold and silver coin. While I was thus engaged, a caravan of merchants came to that neighbourhood, and halted there for a day or two. Taking advantage of this opportunity, I purchased of them sacks for holding the coin, and some strong oxen to carry them. I then dismissed my men, well satisfied with their share, and joined the caravan, where I soon made friends with the leader, the son of a merchant at Oujein, to which place he was then going.

On our arrival at the city, he introduced me to his father, Bandhupāla, by whose means I obtained permission from the King of Mālwa to reside there.

When I had taken a house, safely deposited the money, and established my parents in it, I was anxious to set out again in search of you.

Bandhupāla, seeing this, said to me: "You have already spent much time in searching for your friend, and may spend much more in the same manner to no purpose, if you have no clue to guide you. Now I am skilled in augury and the language of birds; it is probable that I may obtain some indications for you; wait, therefore, patiently for the present. Meanwhile, my house is always open to you."

To this I agreed, and having great pleasure in his society, was much with him, and soon had other attractions there, for I fell in love with his beautiful daughter, Bālachandrika.

Though I had not declared my passion, I

was convinced, from her looks and from many things which I observed, that she was equally in love with me, and therefore anxiously sought an opportunity of speaking to her in private.

One day, Bandhupāla, wishing to obtain information about you by listening to the voices of birds, went with me into a park near the city, and while he waited under the trees, hearing the birds, I walked on, and had the good fortune to see my beloved alone, in another part of the park.

Although she was evidently pleased at seeing me, and did not reject my suit, I observed that she was distressed and dispirited, and inquired the cause.

She told me, "Some time ago the old king abdicated in favour of his son Darpasāra, who is now gone on a pilgrimage to the Himālaya

Mountains, having first appointed as joint regents the two sons of his father's sister, Charmavarma and Dāruvarma.

"The former of these two alone has the management of affairs; for the latter, given up to evil deeds, makes use of his power only for the indulgence of his licentious passions.

"He has seen me during my attendance on the Princess Avantisundari, has endeavoured to seduce me, and I am in constant fear of his violence, for he hesitates at nothing in the indulgence of his wicked desires."

She told me this reluctantly, and with much agitation; but I comforted her with the assurance of my love, and the promise of finding some means to free her from his annoyance.

After some reflection, I said to her, "This is the plan which I propose. Your friends must give out in public that a certain Siddha has declared—'Bālachandrika is guarded by a demon, who will allow no man to have intercourse with her without his consent. Whoever, therefore, wishes to marry her, must first pass one night in company with her and one female friend, and if he comes out uninjured, or is able to overcome the demon, he may then safely marry her.'

"If Dāruvarma, on hearing this, shall be alarmed, and abstain from further annoyance, so much the better; if, on the other hand, he persists in his wicked purpose, do you appear to consent, and say, 'If you think you can overcome the demon, I am willing to meet you, but it must be openly, in your own house; and then, whatever happens, no blame can fall on my family.'

"To this proposal he will be sure to agree,

and you may go to his house without fear, for I will accompany you, disguised as a woman, and will manage to kill that wretch, without danger to you or myself, after which there will be no obstacle to our marriage; for, when I ask your father, he will certainly consent, seeing the great love between us, for he has shown great regard for me, and knows my property and connections. But you must tell him now what has been arranged between us, that he may be induced to spread abroad the report about the demon, and to consent to your going to Dāruvarma's house."

Bālachandrika was delighted with my plan, and promised to do her best to carry it out. She had full confidence in my courage and skill, and felt sure that I should succeed in what I had undertaken. Then, reluctantly leaving me, and looking back again and again, she walked slowly home.

After quitting her I returned to her father, who was well satisfied with the result of his observations, and told me that he had ascertained that after thirty days I should meet you; and we walked together to his house, talking over the matter.

After a few days, Bālachandrika informed me that Dāruvarma, undeterred by the report which was now spread about the city, that she was haunted by a demon, had continued his importunities, and that she had consented to go to his house that evening.

Meanwhile I had secretly made my preparations, and concealed in a lonely place everything required for my disguise. At the proper time, when it was quite dark, I went there, changed my dress, met the lady, and accompanied her to the house of the prince, who received us with great respect; and not having the slightest suspicion of my being other than what I seemed to be, sent away all his attendants, and conducted us to a room in a small detached building. There he seated her on a beautiful soft couch, inlaid with jewels, and expressing his great delight at seeing her, brought forth and offered to us both very handsome presents of dresses, ornaments, perfumes, &c. After some conversation—as if no longer able to restrain himself—he sat down beside her, and, regardless of my presence, threw his arms round her, and kissed her again and again.

This was more than I could bear; suddenly seizing him by the throat, I threw him on the ground, and despatched him with blows of hand, foot, and knee, before he could call out or give an alarm.

Then we both screamed out loudly, and I rushed forth, as if in a great fright, calling out, "Help! help! the horrible demon is killing the prince!"

Hearing this, and seeing my apparent agitation, the attendants and guards hastened in great confusion to the room, where they found the prince dead, and the lady so agitated that she was unable to give an account of what had happened; the demon had of course disappeared.

Some police were in attendance, suspicious of fraud, but even they did not imagine two women to be capable of such an act of violence, and the general opinion was that the story of the demon was founded on truth, and that the prince well deserved the fate he had met with. Bālachandrika was therefore suffered to leave: I had already escaped in the first alarm and confusion, had changed my dress, and reached home in safety.

No further inquiry was made, and no suspicion fell on me; I duly married my beloved, and as no harm happened to me, the demon was supposed to have been propitiated.

The day indicated by my wife's father having arrived, I came here, fully expecting to see you, and now my happiness is complete.

When Rājavāhana had heard this story, he again related his own adventures; after which he took leave of Somadatta, saying, "Come to me as soon as possible, when you have paid your devotions at Mahākāla, and have taken your wife and her attendants home;" and he then accompanied Pushpodbhava into the city of Avanti.

There he was hospitably received in the house of his friend, who introduced him by his real name to Bandhupāla, but gave out in the city that he was a young brahman, worthy of all honour for his learning and ability; and the prince remained for some time in that city, treated with great respect and consideration by all who became acquainted with him.

MARRIAGE OF AVANTISUNDARI.

DURING the stay of Rājavāhana at Avanti, the season of spring arrived, when the great festival of Kāma is celebrated. The trees, breaking into flower, were filled with the song of birds and the hum of bees, and their branches were waved by the soft south wind, blowing, loaded with perfume, from the sandal groves of Malaya. The lakes and pools were thickly covered with lotus blossoms, among which innumerable water-birds were sporting, and the feelings of all were influenced by the charms of the season, and prepared for the worship of the god of love.

On the day of the festival, the parks and gardens were crowded with people, some engaged in various sports, some walking about or sitting under the trees, looking at the players.

Among them was the Princess Avantisundari, who was sitting on a sandy spot, under a large tree, attended by her women, especially by her dear friend Bālachandrika, and making offerings to the god of various perfumes and flowers.

The prince also walked in the park with his friend Pushpodbhava; and wishing to see the princess, of whose grace and beauty he had already heard, contrived to approach; and being encouraged by Bālachandrika with a gesture of the hand, came and stood very near her.

Then, indeed, having an opportunity of observing her, he was struck by her exceeding beauty. She seemed to him as if formed by the god of love with everything most beautiful in the world; and, as he gazed, he felt more and more entranced, till almost unconsciously he was deeply in love.

She, indeed, seeing him beautiful as Kāma himself, was almost equally affected, and, pervaded by strong feeling, trembled like the branch of a creeping plant agitated by a gentle wind.

Then he thought, "Never have I seen anything so lovely. She must have been formed by some singular accident, for there is no one like her in the world."

She, indeed, ashamed to look openly at him, and half concealing herself among her attendants, looked at him stealthily from time to time, and while he had all his thoughts fixed on her, was saying to herself, "Who can he be?

Where does he come from? Happy the maidens whose eyes are delighted with such beauty! happy the mother who has such a son! What can I do? how can I find out who he is?"

Meanwhile Bālachandrika, quick in discrimination, perceived the impression they had made on each other; and not thinking it desirable to declare his name and rank before the other attendants, or in such a public place, introduced him to the princess, saying, "This is a very learned and clever young brahman, a friend of my husband, worthy of your notice. Allow me to recommend him to your favourable consideration."

The princess, delighted at heart, but concealing her feelings, motioned to the prince to sit down near her, and gave him betel, flowers, perfumes, &c., through one of her attendants.

Then Rājavāhana, more deeply in love

even than the princess, thought to himself, "There surely must be some reason for this very sudden attraction which I feel towards her. She must have been my beloved wife in a former existence. Perhaps a curse was laid upon us; and now that is removed. If so, the recognition ought to be mutual; at all events I will try what I can do to produce the same feeling in her which exists in my mind."

While he was considering how this might be accomplished, a swan approached the princess, as if expecting to be fed or caressed; and in sport, she desired Bālachandrika to catch it.

Inspired by this circumstance with a happy thought, Rājavāhana said to the princess, "Will you allow me to tell you a short story? There was formerly a king called Samba. When walking one day together with his beloved wife at the side of a small lake in the pleasure-grounds, he saw a swan asleep, just under the bank. Having caught it, he tied its legs together, put it down again on the ground, and saying to his wife, 'This bird sits as quiet as a muni; let him go where he likes,' amused himself with laughing at its awkward attempts to walk. Then the swan suddenly spoke: 'O king, though in the form of a swan, I am a devout brahman; and since you have thus, without cause, ill-treated me while sitting quiet here, engaged in meditation, I lay my curse upon you, and you shall endure the pain of separation from your beloved wife.'

"Hearing this, the king, alarmed and distressed, bowed respectfully to the ground, and said, 'O mighty sage, forgive an act done through ignorance.'

"Then that holy person, having his anger appeased, answered, 'My words cannot be made of no effect. I will, however, so far modify the curse that it will not take place during your present existence ; but in a future birth, when you are united to the same lady in another body, you must endure the misery of separation from her for two months, though you will afterwards enjoy very great happiness with her ; and I will also confer on you both the power of recognising each other in your next existence,'—I beg of you therefore not to tie this bird which you were wishing to catch."

The princess, hearing this story, was quite ready to believe it ; and from her own feelings was convinced that it really referred to a previous existence of herself, now brought to her recollection ; and that the love which she felt springing up in her heart was directed towards one who had formerly been her husband. With a sweet smile, she answered : " Doubtless

Samba tied the bird in that way on purpose to obtain the power of recognition in another birth; and it was very cleverly managed by him."

From that moment they seemed perfectly to understand each other, and sat without speaking, their hearts full of happiness.

Presently the mother of the princess—the queen of the ex-king Mānasāra, who had also come with her attendants into the park, joined her daughter; and Bālachandrika having seen her approaching, made a sign to the prince, upon which he and his friend slipped on one side, and hid themselves behind some leafy bushes.

After the queen had stayed a short time talking to her daughter and looking at the games, she set out to return, and the princess accompanied her.

Before going, she turned round, as if addressing the swan, but intending the speech for the prince, who was anxiously watching her from his hiding-place, "Though you came near me so lovingly just now, I may not stay longer with you: I must leave you and follow my mother: do not forget me or imagine that I neglect you, for I am still fond of you."

With these words she walked slowly away, looking with longing eyes in the direction of her lover.

On their return to the palace, the princess heard from Bālachandrika a full account of Rājavāhana and his adventures, through which she was even more in love than before; and having no opportunity of seeing him again, became listless and indifferent to her usual occupations, lost her appetite, wasted away, and at last lay on her bed, burning with fever.

In vain did her devoted attendants use all their efforts to diminish the heat by means of cold water, fanning, and other remedies; and she, seeing their distress, said to her faithful Bālachandrika: "Ah, dear friend, all you can do is to no purpose; they call Kāma the god with five arrows; but surely this is a wrong name, for I feel as if pierced by him with hundreds of arrows. They call the wind from Malaya cooling; but to me it only increases the fever, as if blowing up the fire which consumes me: my own necklace, the contact of which was formerly agreeable, now feels as if smeared with the poison of serpents. Give up your exertions; the prince is the only physician who can cure me; and how can he come to me here?"

Then Bālachandrika thought to herself: "Something must be done, and that without delay, or this violent passion of love will surely cause her death. I will at least see the prince, and try if it is possible to bring about a meeting."

Having thus resolved, she begged the princess to write a few lines to her lover; and committing her to the care of the other attendants, she went to the house of her husband. There she found Rājavāhana almost in the same state as the princess, burning with fever, throwing himself about restlessly on his couch, and bemoaning his hard fate to his friend.

On seeing Bālachandrika, he started up, saying, "Oh, how welcome is the sight of you! I am sure you must be the bearer of good news. Sit down here and tell me about my darling."

She answered: "The princess is suffering like yourself, longing to see you; and has now sent me with this letter."

Eagerly opening it, he read—

"Beloved—Having seen your beauty, delicate as a flower, faultless, unrivalled in the world, my heart is full of longing. Do you likewise make your heart soft."

Having read this, he said: "Your coming here is refreshing to me as water to a withered plant; you are the wife of my very dear friend, Pushpodbhava, and I know how attached you are to my darling, therefore I can speak freely to you. Tell her that when she left the grove that day she carried off my heart with her, and that I long to see her even more than she longs for me; tell her only not to despond; the entrance to her apartments is indeed difficult, but I will contrive to see her by some means or other. Come back soon, and, having thought over the matter, I will tell you what is to be done."

With this message, Bālachandrika went to rejoice her friend; and the prince, though much comforted, could not remain quiet, but walked to the park, to have the pleasure of seeing at least the place where he had first met his charmer. There he stayed a long time together with his friend, looking at her footsteps in the sand, the withered flowers which she had gathered and thrown down, the place where she had sat, and the shrubs from which he had watched her, and listening to the murmur of the wind among the leaves, the hum of the bees and the song of the birds. Presently, they saw approaching them a brahman, splendidly dressed, followed by a servant. He, coming up to the prince, saluted him; and the prince, returning the salute, asked who he was. He answered: "My name is Vidyeswara. I am a famous conjurer, and travel about exhibiting my skill for the amusement of kings and nobles. I have now come to Oujein, to show off my skill before the king." Then, with a knowing smile, he added, "But what makes you look so pale?"

Pushpodbhava, thinking to himself this is just the man to help us, answered, "There is something in your appearance which induces me to look on you as a friend, and you know how sometimes intimate friendship arises from a very short acquaintance; I will therefore tell you why my friend is thus sad. Not long ago, he, the son of a king, met the Princess Avantisundari on this very spot, and they fell in love with each other. From the impossibility of meeting, both are suffering, and the prince is brought into this condition which you see."

Vidyeswara, in reply, looking at the prince, said, with a smile, "To such as you, with me for an ally, nothing is impossible. I will, through my skill, contrive that you shall marry the princess in the presence of her father and his court; but you must follow my directions exactly, and she must be informed of her part in the affair through some trusty female friend."

Then, having given the necessary directions, the conjurer went his way. Rājavāhana also returned to the house, and when he had given Bālachandrika, who came again in the evening, the directions received from the conjurer, and a loving message of encouragement for the princess, he anxiously awaited the morrow, unable to sleep from the thought of the expected happiness, and fluctuating between alternate hopes and fears.

In the morning, Vidyeswara, having collected a large troop of followers, went to the palace and announced himself to the doorkeeper, saying, "Tell the king the great conjurer is arrived." Mānasāra, who had heard of his great skill, and was desirous of seeing it, ordered him to be immediately admitted, and, after the usual salutations, the performance began.

First, while the band was playing, peacocks' tails were waving, and singers imitating the plaintive notes of birds, to excite the feelings and distract the attention of the hearers, the conjurer turned round violently several times, with his eyes half-closed, and caused great hooded serpents to appear and vultures to come down from the sky to seize them.

After this, he represented the scene of Vishnu

killing Hiranyakasipu, chief of the Asuras, to the great astonishment of the spectators; thén, turning to the king, he said, "It is desirable that the performance should end with something auspicious; I propose, therefore, to represent a royal marriage, and one of my people will act as your daughter, another as a prince, endowed with all good qualities. But first I must apply to your eyes this ointment, which will give you preternatural clearness of vision." To all this the king consented.

Meanwhile, the princess had contrived to slip out unobserved, and stood among the conjurer's people. Rājavāhana also stood ready, and the performance began. Thus, under the disguise of a piece of acting, the conjurer, being a brahman, was able to complete the marriage with all proper rites and ceremonies without any suspicion on the part of the king that it was his own daughter whom he saw before him; and the others, also unsuspecting, only admired the skill of the conjurer in making the actress so like the lady whom she represented. When the performance was ended, the conjurer, having been liberally rewarded by the king, dismissed his hired attendants and departed.

In the confusion and excitement caused by the conjurer's performance, Rājavāhana and the princess slipped unnoticed into her apartments, where he was safe, for the present at least, her attendants being all devoted to her, and careful to keep the secret.

He was thus able to enjoy the society of his bride without interruption; to give her a full account of his life and adventures, and to teach her many things of which she was ignorant; so that she became more and more attached to him, and admired his knowledge and eloquence as much as she had before admired his beauty.

FURTHER ADVENTURES OF RĀJAVĀHANA.

THUS the princess, listening with delight and astonishment to the sweet and eloquent words of her husband, and he never tired of contemplating her beauty and enjoying her caresses, lived for some time in the greatest happiness, without care or anxiety for the future.

One night, when both were sleeping, the prince had a remarkable dream. He seemed to see an old swan, whose legs were tied together with lotus fibre, approach the bedside; at that moment he awoke with a feeling of pressure on his feet, and found himself bound with a slender silver chain, bright as the rays of the moon. The princess awoke at the same time, and seeing her husband thus fettered, screamed out loudly in her fright. The attendants in the adjoining apartments, hearing the scream, thought something dreadful must have happened. They rushed into the room, added their cries to hers, and forgetting all their former precautions, left the doors open, so that the guards outside, hearing the clamour, entered and saw the prince.

When about to seize him, they were awed by his dignity, and contented themselves with giving information to the regent, Chandavarma, who, on receiving it, came immediately to the place.

Looking at the prince with eyes burning with the fire of anger, he began to recollect him, and said, "So! this is that conceited brahman who has been deceiving the people; making them believe that he is wonderfully clever; the friend of that fellow the husband of the wicked Bālachandrika, the cause of my brother's death. How is it possible that the princess should have fallen in love with such a paltry wretch, overlooking a man like me? She is a disgrace to her family, and shall soon see her husband impaled on a stake."

Then, with his forehead disfigured by a fearful frown, he continued to abuse the prince; and having tied his hands behind him, dragged him from the room.

Rājavāhana, naturally brave, and encouraged by belief in that former existence the remembrance of which had so wonderfully arisen in his mind, bore all the insults with firmness, and saying to the princess, "Remember that speech of the swan, have patience for two months, and all will be well," submitted quietly to the imprisonment.

When the ex-king and queen were informed of what had happened, they were greatly distressed on their daughter's account, and exerted themselves to save the life of their son-in-law; but the regent, in whom all authority was vested, resisted their entreaties; and only on condition of their resigning some of the few privileges which still remained to them did he consent to defer the execution till he had communicated with Darpasāra, and learned his pleasure on the subject. He confiscated the property of Pushpodbhava, and threw him and his family into prison; and being about to march against the King of Anga, and unwilling to leave the prince behind, lest he should be liberated by the old king, he caused a wooden cage to be made, in which his prisoner was shut up and carried with the army.

Treated thus like some wild beast, roughly shaken and neglected, Rājavāhana would have suffered greatly had he not been protected by the magic jewel given to him in Pātāla, and which he had contrived to conceal in his hair.

Chandavarma had some time before this asked in marriage Ambālika, the daughter of Sinhavarma, King of Anga, and, indignant at a refusal, was now marching against him, to take vengeance for the insult, and get possession of the princess. Advancing therefore with a large army, he prepared to besiege Champa, the capital city.

Sinhavarma, being of a very impatient and impetuous disposition, would not wait for the arrival of the allies who had been summoned to his assistance, and were then on the march; but throwing open the gates, went forth to meet the enemy.

A terrible battle ensued, in which both kings performed prodigies of valour. At last Sinhavarma was taken prisoner, and his army so completely defeated, that the conqueror entered and took possession of the city without opposition.

Chandavarma, having now the princess in his power, determined to make her his wife at once: he therefore treated her father with more consideration than he would otherwise have done, though he put him in confinement, and caused it to be proclaimed throughout the city that the wedding would be celebrated with much splendour the next morning.

Just then a messenger arrived from Kailāsa, bringing a letter from Darpasāra, in which he had written, "O fool! should there be any pity for the violator of the harem? If the old king, my father, now in his dotage, was foolish enough to favour the criminal for the sake of his worthless daughter, you had no need of his permission, and ought not to have been influenced by him. Let that vile seducer be immediately put to death by torture, and his paramour be shut up in prison till I come."

Chandavarma, who had intended to march against the allies advancing for the assistance of his captive, on receiving these commands, gave orders to his attendants, saying, "To-morrow morning take that vile wretch from his cage, and set him at the palace gate. Have ready, also, a fierce elephant, suitably equipped, which I shall mount immediately after the wedding, to overtake my army in march against the enemy; and as I set out, I will make the elephant trample the life out of that criminal."

Accordingly, the next morning, the prince was brought by the guards to the gate of the palace, and the elephant placed near him.

While he stood there, calmly awaiting death, which now seemed inevitable, he suddenly felt his feet free, and a beautiful lady appeared before him.

She humbly bowing down said : "Let my lord pardon his servant for the injury which she has unconsciously caused. I am an Apsaras, born from the rays of the moon. One day, as I was flying through the air, wearing a white dress, a swan, mistaking me for a lotus flower, attacked me. While struggling to keep off the bird, the string of my necklace broke, and the pearls fell on the grey head of a very holy rishi, bathing in the clear water of a Himālayan lake.

"In his anger, he cursed me, saying: 'O wicked one, for this offence you are condemned to be changed into a piece of unconscious metal.'

"When, however, I entreated forgiveness, he was so far appeased, that he modified the curse, and granted that I should still retain consciousness, and remain as a fetter on your feet for two months only.

"The change took place immediately, and I fell to the ground, turned into a silver chain.

"About this time, Vírasekhara, a Vidyādhara, partly of human descent, had become acquainted with Darpasāra, then performing penance on the great mountain; and thinking he might get assistance from him in a feud in which he was involved, had made an alliance with him, and engaged to marry his sister, the Princess Avantisundari.

"Being desirous of visiting his intended bride, he flew through the air to Avanti. On his way he saw the silver fetter, descended to the ground, picked it up, and continued his flight.

"Having made himself invisible, he entered without difficulty the apartment of the princess, and was astonished and enraged on finding her lying in your arms. His first impulse was to kill you; but some irresistible influence restrained him, so that he contented himself with putting the silver fetter on your feet, and departed without otherwise disturbing you.

"You have, in consequence, suffered all this misery. Now my transformation is ended, and you are so far free; tell me what I can do for you in atonement for the suffering which I have caused?"

The prince, not thinking of himself, said only, "Go at once to her who is dearer to me than life, and comfort her with news of me."

At that moment a great clamour was heard, and some persons, rushing from the interior of the palace, called out, loudly, "Help! help! Chandavarma is murdered! killed by an assassin, who stabbed him as he was about to take the hand of the princess; and that man is now moving about the palace, cutting down all who attempt to seize him."

Rājavāhana, when he heard this, without losing a moment, and before the guards had perceived his feet to be unfettered, with a sudden spring leapt on the elephant intended for his destruction; and having thrust off the driver, urged the beast at a rapid pace, pushing aside the crowd right and left as he went.

Having got into the courtyard, he shouted with a loud voice, "Who is the brave man that has done this great deed, hardly to be accomplished by a mere mortal? Let him come forth and join me; we two united are a match for a whole army."

The slayer of Chandavarma hearing this, came out of the palace, and quickly mounting the elephant, who held down his trunk to receive him, placed himself behind the prince.

Great was their mutual astonishment and joy when they recognised each other, the prince exclaiming, "Is it possible? Is it really you, my dear friend Apahāravarma, who have done this deed?" and the other saying, "Do I indeed see my Lord Rājavāhana?"

Having thus recognised and embraced each other, they turned the elephant round, and passing through the crowd in the courtyard, went into the main street, now thronged by soldiers. Through these they forced their way, employing with good effect the weapons placed on the elephant for the use of Chandavarma.

Before, however, they had gone far, they heard the noise of battle at a distance, and saw the soldiers in front of them scattered in all directions.

Soon they saw coming towards them a very well-dressed, handsome man, riding on a swift elephant. On reaching them, he made obeisance to the prince, saying, "I am sure this is my Lord Rājavāhana;" and then turning to Apahāravarma, said, "I have followed your directions exactly, and hastened on the advancing allies. We have just now encountered and utterly defeated the enemy, so that there is no fear of any further resistance."

Then Apahāravarma introduced the stranger to the prince, saying, "This is my dear friend Dhanamittra, well worthy of your respect and consideration; for he is as brave and clever as he is handsome. With your permission, he will liberate the King of Anga, and re-establish the former authorities; meanwhile, we will go on to a quiet place, and wait there for him and the princes who have come so opportunely to our assistance.

Rājavāhana agreed to this. They went a little further, and dismounted at a pleasant cool bank, shaded by a large banian tree, and close to the Ganges.

When they had been for some time seated

there, Dhanamittra returned, accompanied by Upahāravarma, Pramati, Mitragupta, Mantragupta, Visruta, Prahāravarma King of Mithila, Kāmapāla lord of Benares, and Sinhavarma King of Anga.

The prince, astonished and delighted at such an unexpected meeting, warmly embraced his young friends, and very respectfully saluted, as a son, the elder men introduced by them. Many questions were asked on both sides. After some conversation, Rājavāhana told them his own adventures, and those of Somadatta and Pushpodbhava, and then begged his friends to relate theirs.

Apahāravarma spoke first.

ADVENTURES OF APAHĀRAVARMA.

MY LORD, when you had gone away with the brahman, and we were unable to find you, I wandered about searching for you like the rest of your friends.

One day I heard by chance of a very famous muni, living in a forest on the banks of the Ganges, not far from Champa, who was said to have supernatural knowledge of past and future events.

Hoping to obtain some information about you, I determined to seek him out, and accordingly came here for that purpose. Having found the way to his dwelling, I saw there a miserable-looking man, very unlike the holy devotee whom I had pictured to myself. Sitting down, however, beside this person, I said, "I have come a long way to consult the celebrated rishi Māríchi, having heard that he is possessed of very wonderful knowledge. Can you tell me where to find him?"

Deeply sighing, he answered: "There was, not long ago, such a person in this place; but he is changed—he is no longer what he was."

"How can that be?" I asked.

"One day," he replied, "while that muni was engaged in prayer and meditation, he was interrupted by the sudden arrival of a famous actress and dancer, called Kāmamanjari, who, with dishevelled hair and eyes full of tears, threw herself at his feet.

"Before he had time to ask the meaning of this, a confused crowd of her companions came up, headed by an old woman, the mother of Kāmamanjari, apparently in great agitation and distress.

"When they were all a little quieted, he asked the girl the meaning of her tears, and for what purpose she had come to him.

"She answered, apparently with great respect and bashfulness, 'O, reverend sir, I have heard of your great wisdom, and your kindness to those who are willing to give up the pleasures of this world for the sake of the next. I am tired of the disgraceful life I am leading, and wish to renounce it.' Upon this, her mother, with her loose grey hairs touching the ground, interrupted her, and said, 'Worthy sir, this daughter of mine would make it appear that I am to blame, but indeed I have done my duty, and have carefully prepared her for that profession for which, by birth, she was intended. From earliest childhood I have bestowed the greatest care upon her, doing everything in my power to promote her health and beauty. As soon as she was old enough, I had her carefully instructed in the arts of dancing, acting, playing on musical instruments, singing, painting, preparing perfumes and flowers, in writing and conversation, and even to some extent in grammar, logic, and philosophy. She was taught to play various games with skill and dexterity, and how to dress well, and show herself off to the greatest advantage in public; I hired persons to go about praising her skill and beauty, and to applaud her when she performed in public, and I did many other things to promote her success, and to secure for her liberal remuneration; yet, after all the time, trouble, and money which I have spent upon her, just when I was beginning to reap the fruit of my labours, the ungrateful girl has fallen in love with a stranger, a young brahman, without property, and wishes to marry him and give up her profession, notwithstanding all my entreaties, and representations of the poverty and distress to which all her family will be reduced if she persists in her purpose; and because I oppose this marriage, she declares that she will renounce the world, and become a devotee.'

"The muni compassionately said to the girl: 'You will never be able to endure the hardships of such a life as you propose to lead—a life so different from that to which you have been accustomed. Heaven may be attained by all who duly perform the duties of their station; take my advice then, give up all thoughts of an undertaking which you will never accomplish, comply with your mother's wishes, return with her, and be content with that way of life in which you have been brought up.'

"With many tears, she replied: 'If you will not receive me I will put an end to my wretched life.'

"Finding her so determined, the muni, after some reflection, said to the mother and her companions: 'Go away for the present; come back after a few days; I will give her good advice, and you will no doubt find her tired of living here, and quite ready to return.'

"Thereupon they all went away, and she was left alone with the muni. At first she kept at a distance from him, taking care not to interrupt him in his meditations, but waiting on him unobtrusively, rendering him many little services, watering his favourite trees, and gathering sacred grass, and flowers for offerings to the gods. Then, as he became more accustomed to her, she would amuse him with songs and dances, and at last began to sit near him and talk of the pleasures of love.

"One day, as if in all simplicity, she said: 'Surely people are very wrong in reckoning virtue, wealth and pleasure as the three great objects of life?'

"'Tell me,' he answered, 'how far do you regard virtue as superior to the other two?'

"'A very wise man like you,' she replied, 'can hardly learn anything from an ignorant woman like me; but since you ask, I will tell you what I think. There is no real acquisition of happiness or wealth without virtue; but the latter is quite independent of the other two. Without it, a man is nothing; but if he fully possesses it, he is so purified by it that he may indulge in pleasures occasionally, and any sin connected with them will no more adhere to him than dust to a cloud. Look at all the stories of the amours of the gods. Are they the less worshipped on that account? I think, therefore, that virtue is a hundred times superior to the other two.' With many such specious arguments as these, and by her winning ways, she contrived to make him madly in love; so that, forgetting all his religious duties and former austerities, he thought only how to please her.

"When she perceived this, she said to him: 'Let us stay no longer in the forest, but go to my house in the town, where we can have many more enjoyments.'

"Utterly infatuated, he was ready to do her bidding; and she, having procured a covered carriage, took him in the evening to her own house.

"The next day there was a great festival, at which the king was accustomed to appear in public and converse familiarly with his subjects. On such occasions he would often be surrounded by actresses and dancing girls.

"On that day Kāmamanjari persuaded the muni to put on a gay dress and accompany her to the park where the festival was held; and he, thinking only of her, and miserable if she were away from him even for a short time, consented to go. On their arrival there, she walked with him towards the king, who, seeing her, said, with a smile: 'Sit down here with that reverend man.' And all eyes were directed towards him.

"Presently one of the ladies rose up, and, making a low obeisance to the king, said: 'My lord, I must confess myself beaten by that lady; I have lost my wager and must now pay the penalty.'

"Then a great shout of laughter arose; the king congratulated Kāmamanjari, and presented her with handsome ornaments.

"After this she walked away with the astonished muni, followed by a great crowd, shouting applause.

"Before reaching her own house, she turned round to him with a low obeisance, and said: 'Reverend sir, you have favoured me with your company a long time; it will be well for you to attend now to your own affairs.'

"Not having his eyes yet opened, he started as if thunderstruck, and said: 'My dear, what does all this mean? What has become of the great love which you professed for me?'

"She smilingly answered: 'I will explain it all.

"'One day, that lady whom you saw in the park had a dispute with me as to which was the most attractive. At last she said: "You boast of your powers, forsooth; go and try them on Maríchi. If you can persuade him to accompany you here, then indeed you may triumph; I will acknowledge myself your inferior."

"'This was the reason of my coming to you; the trick has been successful; I have won my wager, and have now no further occasion for you.'

"Bowed down by shame and remorse, the unhappy man slunk back to his hermitage, miserable and degraded, bitterly lamenting his folly and infatuation, but resolved to atone for it by deep repentance and severe penance.

"I am that wretched man; you see, therefore, that I am now quite unable to assist you. But do not go away; remain in Champa. After a time I shall recover my former power."

While he was telling me this sad story, the sun set, and I remained with him that night. The next morning, at sunrise, I took leave of him, and walked towards the city. On my way thither, as I passed a Buddhist monastery, I was struck by the appearance of a man sitting at the side of the road near it. He was extraordinarily ugly; his body naked, with the exception of a rag round his waist; and his face so covered with dirt, that the tears he was shedding left furrows as they rolled down his cheeks.

Moved by compassion, I sat down near him, and inquired the reason of his distress, at the same time adding, "If it is a secret, I do not wish to intrude upon you."

"'My misfortunes are well known,' he answered; 'I can have no objection to telling you if you wish to hear them.' Then he began:

"My name is Vasupālika; but from my ugliness I am generally known as Virūpaka,—the deformed. I am the son of a man of some importance here, who left me a large fortune.

"Among my acquaintance there was a person called Sundaraka, remarkably handsome, but poor. Between us two some mischievous persons strove to excite a rivalry, pitting my money against his beauty and accomplishments.

"One day, in a large assembly, having got up a dispute between us, they said: 'It is not beauty or wealth, but the approbation of the ladies, which stamps the worth of a man; therefore, let the famous actress, Kāmamanjari, decide between you, and agree that she shall say who is the best man.' To this we both assented, and she, having been previously prepared for the part which she was to perform, was brought into the room, and passing by my rival with scorn, sat down by my side, and, taking a garland from her own head, placed it on mine.

"Greatly flattered and delighted by this preference, and blinded by a mad love for her, which I had not ventured to express, I most readily gave myself up to her seductions, and in a very short time she obtained such an influence over me that everything I possessed was at her disposal. Before long, she had so plundered me, and led me into such extravagance, that I was reduced to the most abject poverty, and had nothing I could call my own but this miserable rag which you now see me wear.

"Cast off by her, blamed and reproached by the elder men, laughed at and despised by those who had been my companions in prosperity, I knew not where to turn; and as a last resource I entered this Buddhist monastery, where I obtain a bare subsistence.

"Distressed by the cutting off of my long hair, and by numerous restrictions as to eating, drinking, and sleeping, like a newly-caught elephant; and hearing every day abuse of those gods whom I used to worship; filled with remorse for my departure from the religion of my ancestors; I am utterly miserable and only wish for death."

Having heard this pitiable story, I did what I could to comfort him, and said, "Do not despair; I have heard already of that wicked woman, and think I shall be able to find some means of making her restore to you a part at least of your property."

After leaving him, I went into the city, and finding, from popular report, that it was full of rich misers, I resolved to bring them to their proper condition by taking away their useless wealth.

Occupied by this thought, I went into a gaming-house, where I was much interested and amused by watching the players and observing their tricks, their sleight-of-hand, their bullying or cringing behaviour to each other; the reckless profusion of the winners, the muttering despair of those who had lost.

While overlooking a game of chess, I smiled and made some remark about a bad move of one of the players, upon which his opponent, turning to me with a sneer, said: "No doubt you think yourself very clever, but wait till I have finished off this stupid fellow, and I will play you for any stake you like."

When the game was over, accepting his challenge, I sat down to play, and won altogether sixteen thousand dīnars. Half of this sum I kept for myself, and half I divided between the gaming-house keeper and the players who were present. The latter were loud in praise of my generosity, and of the skill which I had shown in beating that boaster; the former asked me to dine with him, and I often went to his house and became very intimate with him, and obtained from him much information, especially such as had reference to my purpose.

One very dark night, fully directed by him, I set out, determined on robbery, equipped with a dark dress, a short sword, a spade, a crowbar, a pair of pincers, a wooden man's head,* a magic candle, a rope and grappling-iron, a box with a bee in it,† and some other implements.

Selecting a house where I knew there was much money, I made a hole in the wall, and finding all quiet, enlarged it, entered boldly, and carried off much booty.

As I was returning, looking cautiously about me, I came suddenly upon a young

* To be pushed in through opening in a wall, so as to receive any blow which might be given.

† To be let loose that it might put out the lights.

woman, who was much alarmed at seeing me. Perceiving her agitation, I spoke to her kindly, and assured her that I would much rather assist than injure her.

Encouraged by my words, she told me her story: "My name is Kulapālika; I am the daughter of a rich merchant in this city, and was from childhood engaged to the son of another rich man, named Dhanamittra: he, however, being of a very generous disposition, when he had succeeded to his father's property was preyed on by pretended friends and reduced to comparative poverty. Seeing this, my father refused his consent to our marriage, and, in spite of my reluctance, is determined to give me to a rich man, called Arthapati. To escape this marriage, I have slipped out from home by a secret passage, rarely used, and am going to the house of my lover, who is expecting me and will take me away to some other country; pray do not detain me, but accept this." So saying, she put one of her ornaments into my hand. I did not refuse it, but walked by her side, intending to escort her to her destination.

We had, however, only gone a few steps, when I saw coming towards us, at no great distance, a large body of the citizen guard. Without losing a moment, I said to the trembling girl, "Don't be alarmed; say that I have been bitten by a serpent, and I will manage the rest."

By the time they reached us I had thrown myself on the ground, and lay as if insensible, and she stood over me, crying. On being questioned, she answered, with many tears, and in evident distress: "My husband and I, coming from the country, lost our way, and have only lately entered the city. Just now he was bitten by a serpent, and is all but dead. Is there any one among you skilled in charms who can recover him?"

Among the guard there chanced to be a very conceited man, who had often boasted of his skill, and was now delighted to have an opportunity of displaying it. He stood over me while the others waited, and, with many gesticulations, muttered various charms supposed to be efficacious in such a case; but finding all of no avail, said at last, "Ah! it is too late; the poor man is past all remedies: what a pity I did not see him sooner!" Then, joining his companions, who were impatient to be off, he turned to the sobbing girl and said: "He was evidently fated to die; who can prevail over fate? It is useless to lament; nothing more can be done now; wait a little while, and when we come back we will remove the body."

As soon as they were out of sight I rose up, took her to the house of Dhanamittra, and said to him: "I met this lady just now; I have brought her safely here, and now restore the ornament which she gave me in her fright; for, though I am a robber, I would not steal from one like her."

Delighted at seeing her, he answered: "O, sir, you have indeed rendered me a great service in bringing this dear one in safety here; such conduct is very extraordinary in a man of your way of life, and I am quite unable to understand your motives for acting thus. At all events, I am under very great obligation to you; command my services in future."

After some further talk, I asked him:

"Friend, what do you now intend to do?"

"It will be impossible," he answered, "for me to live here if I marry her without her father's consent; I propose, therefore, to leave the town with her this very night."

"A clever man," I replied, "is at home in any place. Wherever he goes he may say this is my country. But, in travelling, many hardships must be endured—hunger, thirst, fatigue, and dangers from men and wild beasts;—how will this tender girl be able to bear them?

"You seem to be wanting in wisdom and forethought in thus abandoning home and country. Take courage! be guided by me, and you shall marry her and live comfortably here. But first we must take her back to her father's house."

To this he consented without hesitation,

and we set out at once. Guided by her, we entered through the secret passage, carried off everything of value, and got away without exciting alarm.

Having hidden our booty in some old ruins, we were going home, when we fell in with some of the city guard. Fortunately, there chanced to be an elephant tied up at the side of the road. We quickly, therefore, unfastened the rope, mounted him, and urged him at full speed; and before the watchmen could recover from their confusion, were out of sight. Halting the elephant close to the wall of a deserted garden, we got over it with the help of the trees growing there, escaped on the other side, and reached home undetected, where we bathed and went to bed.

The next day we walked out carefully dressed, and were amused at hearing an exaggerated account of our adventures of the preceding night, which had caused much alarm and excitement in the city.

I had hoped, by robbing the old man, to prevent the marriage of his daughter with Arthapati. But this hope was frustrated; for the latter was not only willing to take Kulapālika without a dowry, but even made presents to her father; and it was settled that the marriage should take place at the end of a month.

Finding this to be the case, I felt that something more must be done; and having hit upon a plan which I thought would be effectual, I gave Dhanamittra directions how to act.

Accordingly, a few days afterwards, he went to the king, to whom he was previously known, and having asked for a private audience, said: "A very wonderful thing has happened to me, of which it seems right that your majesty should be informed. You have known me as Dhana-mittra, the son of a very rich man. During my prosperity, I was engaged to the daughter of a wealthy merchant; but when I was reduced to poverty, he refused his consent to our marriage, and is now about to give her to another.

"Driven to despair by the double loss of fortune and wife, I went into a wood near the city, intending to put an end to my wretched life.

"There, when in the act of cutting my throat, I was stopped by a very aged devotee, who asked the cause of the rash act.

"'Poverty, and contempt,' I answered.

"'There is nothing more foolish and sinful

than suicide,' he replied. 'A man of sense will endure adversity rather than escape from it in such a manner. Wealth, when lost, may be regained in many ways; but life in none. A broken fortune may be repaired; a cut throat can never be joined again. But why should I preach to you thus? Here is a remedy for your misfortunes. This leather bag will give you abundant wealth. I have used it for assisting the deserving; but now I am old and infirm, and am not long for this world. I give it to you.

"'Go home; if you possess anything wrongfully acquired, restore it to the right owner, and give away the rest of your property to brahmans and the poor. When this has been done, put away the purse carefully; and in the morning it will be found full of gold. Remember that whoever possesses it must comply with these conditions, and that it will yield its treasures only to a merchant like yourself, or to an actress.'

"With these words, he handed me the purse, and immediately disappeared.

"I have now brought the purse to your majesty, to know your pleasure concerning it."

The king, though much astonished, believing the story, told him to keep and enjoy it; and in answer to his entreaty, promised that any one attempting to steal it should be severely punished.

After this, Dhanamittra, making no secret of his acquisition of the purse, disposed of all his property somewhat ostentatiously, leaving himself absolutely nothing but the clothes which he wore; and in the morning, having filled the purse with gold—the proceeds of the robbery—he showed it to his neighbours, who were fully convinced of its magic powers.

The fame of the purse was thus spread abroad; and we were able to account for our newly-acquired wealth, without incurring any suspicion as to the manner of obtaining it.

At this time, for reasons which will presently appear, I induced Vimardaka to enter the service of Arthapati; and directed him to use all possible means to excite his master against Dhanamittra. In this he had no difficulty; for the father of Kulapālika, hearing of his sudden acquisition of wealth, did not even wait to be asked, but of his own accord renewed the former engagement, and rejected Arthapati.

About that time it was publicly announced

that a younger sister of Kāmamanjari—Rāgamanjari by name—would make her first appearance as a dancer and singer. Great expectations having been raised, a large number of spectators, including myself and my friend Dhanamittra, were present at the performance.

I was struck by her beauty the instant she appeared on the stage; but when I heard her sweet voice, and saw her graceful movements, I was perfectly enchanted, and unable to take my eyes off her for a moment.

The performance being ended, she withdrew, followed by the longing eyes and loud applause of the spectators; and giving, as I fancied, a significant look at me.

The next day I was anxious, restless, and unable to eat; and could do nothing but roam about listlessly, or lie on the couch, thinking of her, and making the excuse of a bad headache.

My friend, seeing me in this state, easily guessed the reason of it, and said to me in private: "I know the cause of your uneasiness, and can give you good hopes. That girl is virtuous, whatever her mother and sister may be; and having watched her closely at the performance, I am convinced that she was much struck with you; therefore, if you are willing to make her your wife, there will be no great difficulties to overcome as far as she is concerned; for, resisting all seductions and the persuasions of her wicked mother and sister, she has declared: 'No man shall have me except as a wife; and I must be won by merit, not by money.'

"On the other hand, her mother and sister,

fearing lest she should be withdrawn from the stage, have gone to the king, and obtained, through many tears and entreaties, a decree that if any man shall take the girl, either in marriage or not, without her mother's consent, he shall be put to death like a robber. Therefore, when you have gained her love, you must also obtain the mother's consent; and that can only be done by means of a large bribe; she will not listen to any other inducement."

"I am equal to all this," I answered; "I will win the young lady, and find means to satisfy the old one." And I lost no time in accomplishing my purpose. It was first necessary to make acquaintance with Kāmamanjari, and to this end I found out a woman often employed by her as a messenger, and having gained her over by bribes, sent, through her, a number of small presents, till at last Kāmamanjari was disposed in my favour, and received me at her house. Meanwhile I contrived to have secret interviews with her beautiful sister, who consented to be my wife. As soon as this was settled, I said to Kāmamanjari, "I am desirous of obtaining your mother's consent to my marriage with your sister, who has accepted me. I know that if she ceases to perform, you will lose a large income; and, therefore, offer you in return something better and more certain. Procure for me the desired permission, and you shall have Dhanamittra's magic purse, which I will safely steal for you."

Delighted at the thought of possessing inexhaustible wealth, she agreed to this; the mother's consent was formally given; and on the day of my marriage I secretly handed over the promised purse.

Very soon after, Vimardaka, by my directions, in a large assembly, began to abuse and insult Dhanamittra, who, as if much astonished, said: "What does all this mean? Why should you annoy me? I am not aware that I have ever given you offence."

He answered furiously: "You purse-proud wretch, do you think I will not take my master's part? Have you not robbed him of his intended wife, by bribing her father? Do you think he has no cause for anger against you? His interests are mine; I am ready to risk my life for him, and I will pay you off. Some day you shall miss that purse, the source of the riches with which you are so puffed up." Saying this, he rushed out of the place in a rage; and though nothing was done at the time, his words were not forgotten.

Then Dhanamittra went to the king, and declaring that he had lost the purse, mentioned his suspicion of Arthapati, and the reason for it. He, having heard nothing of what his servant had said, when summoned and asked "Have you a confidential servant named Vimardaka?" answered without hesitation, "Certainly; he is a very trustworthy man, entirely devoted to my interest."

"Bring him here to me."

Thus commanded, he searched everywhere for his servant, but was unable to find him; and for a good reason, for I had furnished the man with money, and sent him to Oujein, to look for you.

The supposed thief having disappeared, his master was put in prison till further evidence could be procured, for no one but those in the secret doubted that he was the instigator of the theft.

Meanwhile Kāmamanjari, anxious to make use of the magic purse, proceeded to fulfil the conditions attached to its use. She went secretly to Virūpaka, and restored the money of which she had robbed him, and then gave away all her furniture, clothes, and ornaments. This, however, she did so incautiously, that attention was drawn to it; upon which Dhanamittra went again to the king, saying: "I suspect that the actress, Kāmamanjari, has got my purse; for though notoriously avaricious, she is giving away everything she possesses, and there must be some strong reason for such a proceeding."

In consequence of this information, she was summoned to appear the next day, together with her mother; and the two women came in great alarm to consult me.

I said to Kāmamanjari: "No doubt you are suspected of having the purse. This suspicion has arisen from your own imprudence, in giving away your property so openly. I much fear that you will have to give it up, and you will be fortunate if you escape without worse consequences. But you must on no account implicate me; for then I should be put to death, all my property would be confiscated, your sister would die of grief, and you would be utterly ruined."

She answered, with many tears: "It is indeed my own fault, but you shall be safe. That niggardly wretch, Arthapati, is known to be intimate with me. I will say that I received it from him; and, as he is already suspected of stealing it, I shall probably be believed."

To this I agreed, and the next day, when questioned, she at first denied all knowledge of the purse, then admitted having received it, but refused to say from whom, and at last, when threatened with torture, confessed, apparently with great reluctance, that Arthapati was the giver; and this being considered sufficient evidence against him, he was condemned to death.

Then Dhanamittra interceded for him, saying: "A decree was formerly made by one of your ancestors, that no merchant or trader should be put to death for theft. I humbly entreat, therefore, that his life may be spared."

To this the king consented, the poor wretch was banished, and all his property confiscated, a portion of it being given to Kāmamanjari, at the earnest entreaty of Dhanamittra, who got back his purse, and shortly afterwards married Kulapālika.

Having thus performed the promise to my friend, I increased my own wealth, and kept up the reputation of the purse by going on with my robberies, and so impoverished the rich misers, that some of them were glad to receive a morsel of food from the beggars to whom they had formerly refused help, and who were now enriched by my liberality.

Still no suspicion fell on me; but fate is all-powerful, and it was decreed that I should be caught at last.

One night, sitting with my charming wife, intoxicated, partly with wine and partly with her sweet caresses, I was seized with madness, and started up, saying: "All the wealth in the city is not too much for you; I will fill the house with jewels for your sake." Then, like a furious elephant who has broken his chain, I rushed out, in spite of her remonstrances, with a drawn sword, and attacked a body of police, who happened to be passing. Shouting out, "This is the robber!" they soon overpowered me, and I fell to the ground.

The shock sobered me at once, and all the horror of the situation into which I had brought myself by my folly came into my mind. I thought to myself, my intimacy with Dhanamittra is well known; suspicion will fall on him; and unless I can turn it off, he, as well as my wife, will be arrested to-morrow; and I quickly formed a plan by which they, and perhaps I myself, might be saved. But no time was to be lost; and as they were about to take me away, I called out to my wife's nurse, Sringālika, who had followed me, "Begone, old wretch! and tell that vile harlot your mistress, and her paramour, Dhanamittra, that she will never see her ornaments, nor he his magic purse again. I care not for life, if I am revenged on those two wretches."

The old woman being remarkably quick-witted, at once understood my object in speaking thus, and very humbly accosting the police said: "Worthy sir, I entreat you to wait a moment, while I ask your prisoner where he has hid the ornaments of my mistress."

To this they assented, and coming to me, she said: "O, sir, your jealousy is without cause; whatever attentions that man may have paid my mistress, she is not to blame. Now that you are taken from her, she will have no means of support, and must go on the stage again. How can she do this without her ornaments? Take compassion on her, and say where you have hid them."

Then, as if my anger were appeased, I answered: "Why should I, who am about to die, harbour resentment? Come close, and I will whisper where I have put them."

In this manner I managed to give her a few hurried instructions. She went away, with many blessings on me, and thanks to the men for their kindness; and I was taken to the king's prison.

At that time the governor of the prison was a very conceited young man, named Kantaka, who had lately succeeded to the office by the death of his father. When I was brought in, looking at me in a very contemptuous manner, he said: "So you are the thief who has committed so many robberies. If you do not give up the stolen property, and especially the magic purse, you shall suffer every possible variety of torture before you are put to death."

I answered, smiling, "Even though I should give up all the other stolen property, I will never let the purse go back to that wretch Dhanamittra, my greatest enemy. You may try all your tortures; you will never get this secret out of me."

Finding the fear of torture to have no effect, the next day he tried promises; and so went on from day to day, with alternate soothing and threatening.

Meanwhile, my wounds were attended to, and I was well fed; so that I had regained my strength when, one day, Sringālika made her appearance, well dressed, and with cheerful countenance.

To my surprise, she was allowed to speak to me in private. She said to me, joyfully: "Your plan has succeeded. As you directed, I went to Dhanamittra and told him, from you: 'You must go to the king, and say, "The magic purse so lately restored has again been stolen by one whom I regarded as a friend—a certain gambler, the husband of the actress Rāgamanjari. He has taken it from spite, being jealous of his wife, to whom, from kindness, I often made presents. He is now in prison for other offences; and if he is put to death immediately, as he deserves, I fear that I shall never recover my purse. I pray, therefore, that he may not be executed before he has confessed where it is concealed. For he admits having taken it; but declares that he will not give it up, unless his life is spared.'" Your friend, admiring your ingenuity, and having full confidence in your resources, immediately went to the king and obtained his request, so that your life is safe for the present.

"Meanwhile, with the help of gifts furnished by my mistress, I have formed an intimacy with the nurse of the Princess Ambālika, and have been introduced by her to the princess, whose favour I have gained by telling her amusing stories, and whom I have induced to feel an interest in the misfortune of my mistress.

"One day, when I was standing near her in the gallery round the court-yard of the palace, Kantaka, having some business or other, passed through below us. Picking up a flower which the princess had dropped, I let it fall on his head; and when he looked up to see from whose hand it came, I managed to make the princess laugh at something which I said; and the conceited fool, thinking that it was she who had dropped it to attract his attention, went away looking quite pleased and confused.

"That same evening I received a present for my mistress, a small basket marked with the signet of the princess, and containing articles of no great value. This I took to Kantaka; and begging him to observe the strictest secrecy, made him believe that the princess had sent it to him. He was even delighted when, another day, I brought him a dirty dress, telling him that she had worn it.

"Finding him quite ready to believe this, and convinced that she was in love with him, I kept up an imaginary correspondence, bringing very loving messages from her, which I invented, and receiving many from him in return, which I took care not to deliver. His presents, of course, I kept for myself.

"In this manner I have raised his hopes very high; and to encourage him still further, I said: 'I have heard from a learned astrologer, with whom I am acquainted, that you have certain marks upon you which indicate that you will one day be a king. This love on the part of the princess tends to the fulfilment of the prediction. You are therefore on the high road to fortune. If you have spirit enough to pursue it, all you have to do now is to obtain a secret interview with the lady; the rest will follow in due time.'

"'But how can I manage this?' he asked. 'The wall of the garden,' I replied, 'communicating with the princess's apartments, is separated from those of the gaol by a space of a few yards only. You could not get over these walls; but you might make an underground passage, and slip in unobserved; and I will take care that there shall be some one to receive and conduct you to the princess. When once with her, you are safe; for all her attendants are attached to her; not one would betray the secret.'

"'But how can I make this underground passage?' he asked. 'I cannot dig it myself, or employ workmen.'

"'Have you no clever thief here,' I replied, 'accustomed to such work?'

"'Well suggested,' he answered. 'I have just the right man.'

"'Who is he?' I said.

"'That man who has stolen the magic

purse,' said he. 'If he will set to work with a good will he will soon dig his way through.'

"'Very good,' I answered. 'You must persuade him by promising to let him go when the work is done. But it would never do for him to be in the secret; therefore, when he has finished, put on his fetters again, and report to the king that he is exceedingly obstinate; that you have tried all other means to make him confess, and that nothing remains but to put him to torture. No doubt the king will give orders accordingly; and you can easily manage so to inflict it that he shall die under it. When he is dead, your secret will be safe; you can visit the princess as often as you like; and, doubtless, in the end the king, rather than disgrace his daughter, will consent to your marriage; and as he has no other child, will make you his successor.'

"With this proposal he was quite delighted; and has been treating you well, that you may have strength for the work. He intends to ask you to begin to-night; and has sent me to persuade you, believing me to be devoted to his interests, and looking forward to some great reward when he has got his wish."

Having heard this from the old woman, I gave her great praise, and said: "Lose no time. Tell him I am quite ready to do the work."

After this, Kantaka came to me, told me what he wanted, and swore a solemn oath that I should be liberated when the work was done; and I, in return, swore to keep his secret.

Then he took off my fetters; I got a bath

and a good dinner, and presently set to work in a dark corner, under the wall. Soon after midnight the work was done, and an opening made into the courtyard of the women's apartments.

Before returning, I thought to myself: "This man has sworn an oath which he intends to break: for the preservation of my own life, therefore, I shall be justified in killing him."

Having formed this resolution, I went back to the prison, where Kantaka was waiting for me. He told me it was necessary to replace my fetters for the present; and I appeared to acquiesce. But as he was stooping to fasten them, I gave him a violent kick; and before he could recover himself, I had snatched a short sword which he wore, and cut off his head.

I then returned to Sringālika, who had remained in the prison, and said to her: "I am not disposed to have had all this toil for nothing. Tell me the way into the ladies' rooms. I will go there and steal something before I make my escape."

Having received her directions, I passed again through the tunnel which I had made, came up into the court-yard, and from thence entered a large, lofty room lighted by jewelled lamps, where a number of women were sleeping.

There, on a couch ornamented with beautifully carved flowers and resting on lions' feet, I saw the princess, covered only by a thin silken petticoat, half sunk into a soft white feather-bed, like lightning on an autumn cloud.

Fast asleep, as if wearied by much play, she lay in a very graceful attitude, with her delicate ancles crossed, her knees slightly drawn up; one lovely hand laid loosely on her side, the other beneath her head; her full bosom, slowly heaved by gentle breathing, illuminated by the ruby necklace strung on burnished gold; the top-knot of her loosened hair hanging down like some graceful flower; her lips so bright that the opening of the mouth could hardly be distinguished; her features in calm repose, shaded by her lovely ringlets.

I had entered so softly that no one was disturbed; and I stood gazing for some time lost in admiration of her beauty, quite forgetting the purpose for which I had come.

I thought, she is, after all, the lady of my heart. If I do not obtain her, Kāma will not suffer me to live; but how can I make known my love to her? Were I now to wake her, she would start up with a cry of alarm, and I should probably lose my life. I must think of some other way of letting her know my love.

Then, looking round, I saw laid on a shelf a thin board prepared for painting, and a box of paints and brushes. With these I made a hasty sketch of the princess as she lay, and of myself kneeling at her feet, and underneath it I wrote this verse :—

> "Of thee thy slave in humble attitude thus prays :
> Sleep on, not worn like me by pervading love."

I then painted on the wall near her a pair of chakravākas in loving attitude, gently took off her ring, replacing it with mine, and slipped out without disturbing any of the sleepers.

There was at that time among the prisoners a man named Sinhaghosha, formerly a chief officer of police, but now imprisoned through a false accusation made by Kantaka.

With this man I had already made acquaintance, and I now went to him and told him how I had killed Kantaka. With his consent I went forth from the prison, and walked away with Sringālika. We had not gone far when we fell in with a patrol. I thought to myself I could easily run away from them; but what would become of the poor old woman? she would certainly be caught. Hastily determining, therefore, on what was best to be done, I walked right up to them with unsteady gait and idiotic look, and said: "Sirs, if I am a thief kill me, but you have no right to touch this old woman."

She, perceiving my intention, came up, and very humbly said: "Honoured sirs, this young man is my son. He has been for some time confined as a lunatic; but was supposed to be cured, and I brought him home yesterday. In the middle of the night, however, he started up, and calling out: 'I will kill Kantaka and make love to the king's daughter,' rushed out into the street. I have at last overtaken him, and am trying to take him home. Will you be so good as to help me, and tie his hands behind him that he may not get away again?"

As she said this, I called out: "O old woman, who ever bound a god or the wind? Shall these crows catch an eagle?" and started off at full speed. She, renewing her entreaties, begged them to pursue me; but they only laughed at her, and said: "Do you think we have nothing to do but to run after madmen? You must be as mad as he is to have taken him out;" and so they went on their way.

I stopped when I found I was not pursued. She soon overtook me, and we went to my house, to the great joy of my wife, who had scarcely hoped for my deliverance.

In the morning I saw Dhanamittra, told him all that had happened, and thanked him for following my directions so punctually.

After this I went to the forest, to see Mārichi. I found him restored to his former condition, and able to give me the desired information. From him I learnt that you would be here about this time.

In the morning after my escape, Sinhaghosha informed the king of what had happened, and how Kantaka had been killed when about to enter the princess's apartments. Being found to be innocent of the crime of which he was accused, he was appointed governor of the prison in Kantaka's place.

Before the underground passage was filled up, he permitted me to pass through it more than once to the princess, who was favourably disposed towards me through the picture and verse, and still more by all that Sringālika had said in my favour.

No great search was made after me, and by keeping quiet and going out only at night I escaped further arrest.

You know how Chandavarma besieged Champa, and how Sinhavarma was defeated and taken prisoner. When I heard this, and how the conqueror intended to force the princess to marry him, I went to Dhanamittra and said: "Do you go about among the ministers and officers of the imprisoned king and the principal citizens, and tell them to be ready to attack the enemy as soon as they hear of the death of Chandavarma. I will engage to kill him to-morrow."

How Dhanamittra has performed his part you have just seen. As to myself, I put on a dress suitable for the occasion, and, as many persons were going in and out of the palace, managed to slip in unobserved and get very near the intending bridegroom. Suddenly stretching out my arm as he was about to take the hand of the princess, I gave him a mortal wound with a sword; then saying a few hasty words of encouragement to her, I defended myself against those who endeavoured to seize me, till I heard your welcome voice, deep as the sound of thunder, and had the happiness of embracing you.

Rājavāhana, having heard this story, said: "You have indeed shown wonderful ingenuity and courage;" then he turned to Upahāravarma, and said: "It is now your turn;" and he, having made due salutation, thus began:—

ADVENTURES OF UPAHĀRAVARMA.

WHILE wandering about like the others, I came one day into the country of Videha. Before entering into Mithila, the capital, I stopped to rest at a small temple, and found there an old woman, who gave me water for my feet.

Observing that she looked at me very hard, and that tears came into her eyes, I asked her: "O, mother, what is the cause of your grief?"

"You bring to my mind," she answered, "the remembrance of my lost foster-child, who, if he lives, is just about your age. But I will tell you how he was lost.

"Prahāravarma was formerly king of this country. His queen was a very dear friend of Vasumati, wife of Rājahansa, King of Magadha, and he went with her and his twin sons to visit that king. How he was conquered and driven from his dominions by the King of Mālwa you have doubtless heard. It was shortly before that invasion that the visit was made. In the battle which was fought, Prahāravarma assisted his friend, and was taken prisoner, but was subsequently liberated.

"When returning to his own kingdom, he heard that a rebellion had broken out, headed by his brother's son, Vikatavarma. He therefore turned aside through a forest road, in the direction of Suhma, hoping to obtain assistance from his sister's son, the king of that country. On the march, he was attacked and plundered by Bheels; and I, having charge of one of his children, was separated from the party, and left behind in the forest.

"There I was attacked by a tiger, and dropped the child. The tiger was killed by an arrow; but I fainted away, and when I recovered, the child was gone, taken away, I suppose, by the Bheels. Having been found and taken care of by a compassionate cowherd, I stayed at his cottage till my wounds were healed.

"Longing to get back to my friends, and to hear some tidings of my mistress, I was surprised one day by the appearance of my daughter, who had been, with me, in charge of the other child.

"After mutual congratulations and embraces, she told me her story as follows: 'After we were parted, I was wounded by the robbers, lost the child, and was found wandering about by one of the foresters, who took care of me, and afterwards wished to make me his wife. I was too much disgusted with him and his way of life to consent; and, after many threats, he would at last have killed me, but for the opportune arrival of a young man who happened to be passing, and rescued me from his hands. That young man has since become my husband. We have been searching for you, and have now happily found you.'

"I asked who the man was. He answered: 'I am a servant of the King of Mithila, to whom I am now going.' Then we all three went to Mithila, and told the king and queen the sad news of the loss of their children.

"The war was still going on, and at last the king was overcome and imprisoned, together with his queen, by his wicked nephew.

"Since then I have been living as a mendicant. My daughter, whose husband was killed in the war, being destitute like myself, has entered the service of Kalpasundari, queen of the usurper. Ah! if those princes had lived, they would have rescued their father from such degradation."

She began then to weep and lament; but I comforted her, and said: "Do you not remember speaking to a certain muni, and telling him of the loss of the child? That boy was found by him. I am he, and I will contrive some means for killing that wicked usurper, and setting my parents free. No one can recognise me here, not even my own mother, were she to see me; therefore I shall be able at my leisure to consider what is best to be done."

Exceedingly delighted at hearing this, she

kissed me again and again, and said, with tears of joy: "O, darling! a glorious fortune is before you. Now you are here, all will be well; you will soon lift up your parents from the sea of sorrow which has engulfed them. Happy is Queen Priyamvada in having such a son!"

Then she gave me such food as she had, and I stayed with her, and passed the night in that temple.

As I lay awake, I turned over in my mind every plan that suggested itself to me for the accomplishment of my purpose. Knowing how ready-witted women are in general, and their fondness for tricks and intrigues, it occurred to me that my foster-sister, from her position near the queen, might be able to give me material assistance.

In the morning, after worshipping the gods,

I began to question the old woman as to her knowledge of the interior of the palace, and asked whether she had frequent opportunities of seeing her daughter. Scarcely had she begun to answer my questions when I saw some one coming towards us, and she exclaimed: "O, Pushkarika, behold our master's son; that dear child whom I so carelessly lost in the forest was found and preserved, and is now restored to us."

Great was the daughter's delight at seeing me; and, when her agitation had subsided, her mother said to her: "I was just beginning to tell my dear son something of the arrangement of the palace, and the habits of the inmates; but you can give him the required information much better than I can."

In answer to this she told me all the arrangements of the palace, and added: "The Queen

Kalpasundari, the daughter of the sovereign of Kumāra, is exceedingly beautiful and accomplished. She despises her husband, who is exceedingly ugly; but though unkindly treated, and neglected, she has hitherto been faithful to him."

Hearing this, I said to her: "Whenever you have an opportunity, dwell on the king's licentiousness; find out, if possible, his scandalous amours; make much of them; tell her how other women have behaved in similar circumstances; in short, do everything to stir up her indignation and jealousy against him; and, as soon as possible, let me know what she says. You may help me greatly in this affair; therefore be diligent and observant, and be as much as possible with your mistress."

Then I said to the old woman: "You must

also play your part. You can be introduced to the queen as a woman skilled in charms and fortune-telling. When you get her to listen to you, make the most of the opportunity, and second your daughter's endeavours."

They both promised to do their utmost. After they were gone I took a small house, close to the wall of the royal gardens, and waited patiently for the result.

After some days the old woman came to me, and said: "Darling, we have done exactly as you wished. The queen has taken a great fancy to me, is very indignant with her husband, and thinks herself greatly to be pitied. What is now to be done?"

I then painted a portrait of myself, and said: "Show this to the queen; she will no doubt admire it, and say: 'Is this a portrait or a fancy picture?' Then do you answer: 'Suppose it should be a portrait of some living person; what then?' And whatever she says in reply let me know as soon as possible."

The next day she came to me again, and said: "When I showed your portrait to the queen, she gazed at it a long time, and seemed lost in admiration; then she exclaimed, 'Who can have painted this? Is it possible that such a handsome man can exist in the world? Surely there is no one here like this!' I answered, 'O lady, your admiration is quite natural, such a handsome man is very rarely to be found, but still there might be such a one; and if this should be really the portrait of a young man, longing to see you—not only thus handsome, but of good birth, very learned, accomplished, and good-tempered—what would you say then?' 'What would I say? I say, that if he will be mine, all that I can give him in return, myself, my heart, my body, my life, will be all too little. But surely you are only deceiving me; there never can be such a charming person as this picture represents.'

"In answer to this, I said: 'I am not deceiving you. There is really such a person, a young prince, who is staying here in disguise; he saw you when you were walking in the public park, at the feast of Spring, and immediately became a mark for the arrows of Kāma. Moved by his entreaties, and seeing how suited you are to each other, I have ventured to take this means of making his passion known to you. If you will but consent to see him, however difficult access to you may be, his courage, prudence, and ingenuity are so great, that he will certainly effect it;

only say what your pleasure is.' Then, finding her quite disposed to see you, I told her your real name and birth. After reflecting some time, she said, 'Mother, I will not conceal from you a circumstance which his name brings to my memory. My father was a great friend of the deposed king, and their queens were very much attached to each other. It was settled between them, that if the one had a son, and the other a daughter, the two children should be engaged for marriage; but when the Queen Priyamvada had lost her sons, my father gave me in marriage to Vikatavarma. This young prince was really destined to be my husband, and I ought to have had him, instead of that ugly wretch, who is stupid, ignorant of all the arts of pleasing, brutal, rebellious, cruel, boastful, false, and, above all, most insulting in his behaviour to me;

only yesterday he ill-treated my favourite attendant, Pushkarika, and gathered flowers from a plant which I had especially cherished, to give to one of his paramours, a low vulgar woman, who is trying to put herself on an equality with me. He is in every way unsuited to me, and my misery is so great, that I am ready to catch at any means of escape from it. It was wretched enough while I thought on no one else, but now that I have heard of this charming young man, and seen his portrait, I will endure it no longer, whatever the consequences may be. Therefore, let him come to-morrow evening to the Mādhavi bower in the garden. I am impatient to see him; even the hearing of him has filled my heart with love.'"

When the old nurse had given me this account, I determined to risk the adventure, and obtained from her a minute description of the garden, the direction of the road and paths, the exact situation of the summer-house where I was to meet the queen, and where the guards were stationed.

Having carefully impressed all these details on my memory, I waited impatiently for the following night, and lay down to rest. As I lay I thought on the difficulty of the enterprise, of the sin of seducing the wife of another, and of what Rājavāhana and my other friends would say to such conduct. On the other hand, I seemed to be justified by the object I had in view, the liberation of my parents.

Perplexed with these conflicting thoughts I fell asleep, and dreamed that Vishnu appeared to me, and said: "Go on boldly, without hesitation; what you are about to do, though it may seem sinful, is approved of by me." Encouraged by this vision, I rose in the morning, fully confirmed in my purpose. The tedious day came at last to an end, and darkness set in.

When the proper time arrived, I put on a close-fitting dark dress, girded on my sword, and set out on the dangerous enterprise.

Concealed at the edge of the ditch, I found a long bamboo, which the old woman had procured for me. This I laid across, and so got to the bottom of the wall. Then, cautiously raising it, I climbed to the top, just where a large heap of bricks had been piled up inside. Using these as steps, I got safely to the ground, and walked northward, through an avenue of champaka trees, where, as a favourable omen, I heard the low murmuring cry of a pair of chakravākas.

Taking an almost opposite direction, I saw before me what appeared to be a great building, and it was only by touching it that I found it to be a clump of trees. Going eastward, and turning once more to the south, I passed through some mango trees, and saw the light of a lantern shining among the leaves. I then knew that I was right, and went straight up to the bower, inside of which was a summer-house, with steps leading up to it, and spread with soft twigs and flowers for a carpet. The room was furnished with a handsome couch, a golden water-jar, trays of flowers, fans, &c. After I had been seated a short time, I heard the tinkling of ornaments and smelt a powerful perfume. Rising up hastily, I slipped out, and stood concealed by the shrubs outside. Presently I saw the lady enter; she looked about her, and not seeing me, was evidently disappointed and distressed. I heard her say, with a sad low voice, "Alas! I am deceived, he is not coming; O my heart, how can this be borne? O adorable Kāma, what have I done to offend thee, that thou thus burnest me and dost not reduce me to ashes?"

Having heard this, I made my appearance, and said: "O lovely lady, do you ask how you have offended Kāma? You have given him great offence, since you disparage his beloved Rati by your form, his bow by your arched eyebrows, his arrows by your glances, his great friend, the perfumed wind of Malaya, by your sweet breath, the notes of his favourite bird by your voice. For all this Kāma justly torments you. But I have done nothing to offend him; why should he so distress me? Have pity on me, and cure the wound inflicted by the serpent of love, with the life-giving antidote of an affectionate look."

Delighted at seeing me, she required no entreaty on my part, and readily yielded to my embrace; and, sitting down on the couch, we conversed as though we had been long acquainted.

At last the time for separation arrived, and I rose up to go; but she with tears detained me, saying: "When you depart, my life seems to follow. If you go, let me go with you."

I answered: "O my beloved, that is impossible. If you love me, be guided by me, and we shall soon meet again, not to be parted."

This she readily promised, and I told her exactly what was to be done. Then quitting her with reluctance, I returned safely by the way I had come, and she went back to the palace.

The next day she showed the picture to the king, who greatly admired it, and asked her where she had got it. She told him: "I have lately made acquaintance with a very wonderful old woman, who has travelled over many countries and seen many strange things; she is very skilful in charms, and has brought me this picture, saying: 'It has very great magical powers, and so confident am I in their efficacy that I ask for no payment or reward until you have fully proved them.' She tells me that if certain ceremonies are performed, and mantras which she has taught me, are recited in a retired spot at midnight, I shall be changed to a person exactly resembling the portrait, and shall have the power of transferring that form to you while I regain my own shape.

I have thought it right to tell you this; but do not act hastily: show the picture to your ministers and consult them."

The king, greatly astonished, but very desirous of obtaining such a handsome body, asked the opinion of his counsellors and younger brothers, and they saw no reason why the experiment should not be tried.

The hour of midnight on the day of full moon was therefore appointed for the ceremony, and there was much talk in the city about it.

"O the wonderful power of magic! Through the skill of the queen, the king will obtain a new body fit for a god."

"But is there no danger?"

"How can there be danger when the ceremony is to be performed by his own queen, in his own private gardens, where no stranger can enter? Besides, have not the learned and clever ministers and counsellors approved of it, and is it likely that they would be deceived?"

The city was full of such talk as this, and the people awaited with impatience the night appointed for the working of the miracle.

When the time arrived a great heap was made in a part of the garden where four roads met, not far from the summer-house, with large quantities of sandal-wood, lignaloes, and other sweet-smelling woods, camphor, silk dresses, sesamum, saffron, and various spices; and several animals, duly slaughtered by the priests, were laid upon it; and the fire having been lighted, every one withdrew except the king and queen. She then said to him: "You know how faithless you have been to me, and with this handsome body you will be a much greater attraction to other women. I know the fickleness of your disposition. Can you expect that I will confer on you this beauty for the sake of my rivals?"

Then he threw himself at her feet, and said: "O my darling, forgive my transgressions. I swear by everything solemn that in future I will keep to you only, and not even think of any other woman."

After these and many other protestations, she appeared to be satisfied, and said: "Now withdraw to that clump of trees, and stay there till I ring the bell; then you may come again to the fire and see the wonderful change in me."

Meanwhile, under cover of the thick smoke arising from the burning of all those substances, I had climbed the wall as before, and was standing in the summer-house when the queen came in. She said: "Everything is ready. I regard myself now as entirely yours; nothing shall part us any more;" and, throwing her arms round my neck, she kissed me again and again.

Saying to her, "Stay here concealed while I finish the work," I quitted her, went to the place of sacrifice, and rang a bell hanging on a neighbouring tree; and the sound summoned the king, like a messenger of death.

He found me standing by the fire, throwing on it more sandal-wood, lignaloes, and other precious things; and as he stood gazing in fear and astonishment, and hardly believing his eyes, I said to him: "Remember what you have promised, and now swear to me again, taking this sacred fire as a witness, that you will renounce all other women, and keep to me only."

He answered: "O queen, there is no deceit in me. I will do all that I have promised," and he repeated his former oaths.

But as if not satisfied with this, I said: "I must have some other proof of your sincerity. Tell me some of your state secrets."

Then he told me: "My father's brother, Prahāravarma, has been for a long time in prison; with the consent of my ministers, I intend to poison him, and give out that he has died of old age and infirmities.

"I am preparing an army, to be commanded by my brother, for the invasion of Pundra without any declaration of war.

"There is a merchant here possessed of a diamond of immense value. I am contriving a plan by which I shall get it from him at a tenth of its worth.

"There is a man of wealth and influence very displeasing to me. I have engaged a certain person, named Satahali, the governor of the district, to bring a false accusation against him, and by that means to stir up the people, and so cause his death in a popular tumult, which will take away all blame or suspicion from me."

When I had heard all these things, saying, "Die the death which your wicked deeds deserve," I suddenly seized him by the throat, stabbed him in a moment to the heart, and threw the body into the great fire, where it was quickly consumed; after which I went back to the queen, who was anxiously awaiting me. Though much agitated, she was more relieved at having got rid of that wretch than shocked at the manner of his death; and having quieted and consoled her without much difficulty, I went at once with her to her apartments.

On seeing him, whom they believed to be the king, so changed, the women and attendants who met us were evidently much astonished, but so much had been said beforehand about the wonderful transformation to be expected, that no one seemed to doubt that I was really the king with a new body; and having said a few words of encouragement to them, I was received with great respect.

The rest of the night was passed in hearing from the queen as much as possible about the court, the ministers, &c., so that I might not appear to be ignorant of what the king must have known, when I should meet them on the morrow.

In the morning, after the performance of due worship of the gods, I met the ministers in council, and they also were so convinced of the power of magic that they did not hesitate to acknowledge me as their master, expressing their delight at the happy change.

Then I said to them: "With this new body I have new feelings and purposes. I repent of my cruelty to my uncle, and instead of getting rid of him as I had intended, it is my pleasure that he shall be taken from prison and treated with all proper respect.

"That diamond, of which I had intended to get possession, must not be obtained by fraudulent means. If I should decide on having it, I will pay the full price."

To the brother who had been appointed to command the army, I said: "Dear brother, our purpose is changed with regard to that invasion. You will only watch the frontier; and if there is any beginning of war on the part of the Pundras, attack them vigorously; but not otherwise."

I sent also for Satahali, and said: "You know that I wished to get rid of Anantasíra, because he was suspected of being a partisan of the deposed king. Now that I am reconciled to my uncle, there is no occasion for anything to be done to him; you will therefore take no further steps in that affair."

When the ministers heard all this, and perceived me to be acquainted with secrets known only to the king and themselves, they were quite confirmed in their first impression; and while congratulating me and the queen, were loud in their praise of the power of magic.

My parents were immediately liberated from prison; and having been informed by the old nurse of what had been done by me, were quite prepared when I went to them in public; and afterwards, when we met in private, were able to give way to their feelings of affection and delight at seeing me again.

After a short time, with the consent of my wife, I resigned the crown, and reinstated my parents in their former position; retaining for myself the dignity of heir-apparent.

Soon afterwards, a letter arrived from Sinhavarma, an old friend of my father's, congratulating him on his restoration, and asking for help against Chandavarma, who was marching to attack him. Upon which I hastily equipped an army, and marched to his assistance; and have now had the great happiness of meeting with you, as well as of helping to defeat the enemy.

Rājavāhana having heard this story, smiled, and said: "Truly, our friend here has committed great sins; but how can I blame him when his motives were so good, and he had the praiseworthy object of liberating from a long imprisonment those who are so dear to him, and of punishing the usurper and oppressor? His courage and ingenuity have been great; and I congratulate him on his success."

Then turning to Arthapāla, he said: "Do you relate your adventures." And he immediately began his story in the following manner:—

ADVENTURES OF ARTHAPĀLA.

MY LORD, having the same object as your other friends, I wandered about over various countries in search of you. In the course of my travels, I arrived one day at the sacred city of Benāres. There I bathed in the pure crystal water of the river; and duly worshipped the mighty god, the slayer of Andhaka, at his temple outside the city. After finishing my devotions, I was going on my way, when I saw a tall, stout man, carrying an iron club, with his eyes red and swelled from weeping, and engaged in making a noose with his sash.

I thought to myself: "This man has

fallen into some great calamity. He is thinking of doing violence to himself or to others. I will see if I can assist him." I therefore went up to him, and said: "This conduct of yours seems to indicate some rash purpose. May I know the cause of your grief? Perhaps I may be able to help you."

He hesitated for a moment, and looked very hard at me; but at last he said: "What harm can there be in telling you? You shall know my troubles, if you wish to learn them."

Then we sat down together under a shady tree, and he began his tale as follows:

"O, fortunate sir, I was once as happy as you appear to be. My father was in good circumstances, and brought me up carefully; but I preferred a wild, dissipated life, and at last became a robber. One night I broke into the house of a rich man in this city, was caught in the act, and condemned to death.

"My hands were fettered by being passed through holes in a heavy piece of wood; and in this state I was led out for execution into a public square, where a furious elephant was brought forward to trample me to death. When he came near me, I shouted as loudly as possible, in order to frighten him; and lifting up my arms, gave him a violent blow on the trunk. Upon this, he turned away; and as I continued to shout out and abuse him, all the efforts of the driver to make him attack me were in vain.

"Again and again, with much difficulty, the driver brought him in front of me; but each time, instead of attacking me, he turned back, alarmed by my menacing appearance and loud shouts; and at last ran right away, leaving me uninjured.

"The courage which I had shown was observed by the king's chief minister, Kāmapāla, who was looking on from one of the towers of the palace; and he sent for me, and said: 'You seem to be a very strong, brave man. I did not think that elephant could have been so cowed by any one. It is a pity that such qualities should not be better employed. Are you willing, if you are pardoned, to forsake your evil ways, and lead an honest life? If you will give me a promise to this effect, I will take you into my service.'

"I gladly gave the promise which he required; and he obtained my pardon, and became my protector and master; and I have served him faithfully ever since. After some years, seeing my devotion to him, he placed great confidence in me, and one day told me his own history.

"'There was,' said he, 'formerly at Pushpapuri a very learned and pious man, named Dharmapāla, one of the king's ministers. His eldest son was like him; but I, the youngest, was of a very different disposition. I had no inclination for work or study; but thought only of amusement, and spent my time among gamblers and disreputable characters. My father and brother did all they could to restrain me; but, impatient of their control, I left my home and friends, and wandered about the world. One day I came to this city, Benāres, and not long after my arrival, I made acquaintance with the king's daughter, who, with her female friends, was playing at ball in a park outside the town. We fell in love with each other; and I contrived, by disguising myself as a woman, to enter her private apartments and to have many secret meetings with her; the result of which was the birth of a child.

"'The devoted attendants kept the whole affair secret, removed the infant as soon as it was born, and telling the mother it was dead, gave it to a savari woman, who carried it to the public cemetery and left it there.

"'As she was returning, she was stopped by the watchmen, and in her fright told them what she had done. Information was given to the king, and further inquiry being made, my offence was discovered, and one night I was arrested, while quietly sleeping unsuspicious of danger. Being condemned to death, I was led to execution outside the city. By a fortunate chance I got my hands free, and snatching the sword from the executioner, laid about me so vigorously that all the men fell back, and I made my escape to the forest. There I wandered about for some time, subsisting on wild fruits and roots, and sleeping in the trees.

"'While living this precarious life, I was one day astonished at meeting a young lady, with many female attendants. She addressed me by my name, and desired me to sit down with her, under a large tree.

"'When, with much surprise, I asked who she was, and how she came to be in that wild forest, with such a retinue, and why I was so favoured by her, she told me the reason of her coming, saying: My name is Tārāvali. I am the daughter of a chief Yaksha. A short time ago I went to visit a friend, living on the Malaya Mountains, and while flying through the air on my return, as I passed over the cemetery of Benāres, I heard the cry of a child.

"'Moved with compassion, I alighted on the ground, took it up and carried it to my father. He took it to our master, the god Kuvera, who sent for me, and asked, "What induced you to bring this child?" "A strong feeling of compassion," I answered, as if it had been my own.

"'You are right,' he replied; 'there is good reason for what you have done;' and he showed me how, in a former existence, when you were Sudraka and I Aryadāsi, the child, now born of the Princess Kantimati, was ours; therefore, I am really your wife, and it was indeed a maternal instinct which prompted me to save the infant. Kuvera, however, would not allow me to keep the boy, but ordered me to take him to the Queen Vasumati, that he might be brought up together with her son, who will one day become a great monarch.

"Having performed the command of the god, I am permitted by him to find you out, and relieve you from your present distress."

"So saying, she embraced me, and afterwards took me to a fairy palace in the forest, furnished with all comforts and luxuries, where I passed some time with her in great happiness.

"One day, when she was expressing her great love for me, I said: 'I have a strong desire to take some vengeance on the king who would have put me to death.' Upon which, with a smile, she said, 'Ah! you wish to see Kantimati; I am not jealous, I will take you to her.'

"Then lifting me up, she bore me through the air to the palace, and without disturbing the guards, placed me at the bedside of the king.

"Grasping a sword lying near him, I awakened him, and said: 'I am your son-in-law; I took your daughter without your consent, and am now come to make submission and atone for my fault.'

"Seeing the drawn sword held over him he was much alarmed, and said: 'I must have been mad to act as I did and reject such a son-in-law; I will now acknowledge you, and you shall duly marry my daughter.'

"He kept his word, the next day announced the intended marriage to all the court, and shortly afterwards publicly gave me his daughter.

"Tārāvali remained with me, became great friends with her fellow-wife, told her the story which she had related to me, and how her son had been preserved and was taken care of by Queen Vasumati.

"Thus I have for some years lived happily, holding, as you know, a very important office."

[End of the story of Kāmapāla as told to his servant.]

"Some time after this, the death of the old king occurred, and as the eldest son had died during his father's lifetime, of consumption brought on by dissipation and debauchery; my master, together with the other ministers, placed Sinhaghosha, a boy about five years old, on the throne, and had him carefully educated.

"As the young king grew older, he was surrounded by companions nearer his own age, and they not liking the restraint put upon them by the wise and prudent Kāmapāla, endeavoured secretly to excite a prejudice against him, saying, 'This fellow, who sets himself up to be so wise and virtuous, is a wicked wretch, who first seduced the princess, and then, having escaped the death he so well deserved, managed to get to the bedside of the sleeping king, and to frighten him into compliance with his demands. This Kāmapāla intends to make himself king; he poisoned your eldest brother, and only spared you in order to obtain the support of the people, knowing that the real power would remain in his own hands. Depend on it you will not be suffered to live when you are old enough to shake off his authority. If you wish to be safe you should get rid of him at once.'

"With these, and other similar speeches, they so prejudiced the young king against his guardian and minister, that he would gladly have got rid of him at once, but was deterred by fear of the power of his Yaksha wife.

"One day the queen, seeing the Princess Kantimati very sad, asked her the reason of her sadness, saying, 'Tell me the truth; you cannot deceive me; what is the cause of this depression?' 'Did I ever deceive you?' she answered; 'my friend and fellow-wife, Tārāvali, has taken offence at something done or said by our husband, and though we tried to soothe her, she went away, and has not returned; this is the cause of my distress.'

"The queen hearing this, immediately told

her husband, 'Kāmapāla has quarrelled with his fairy wife, and she has left him. There is nothing now to prevent your proceeding against him as you please.'

"Sinhaghosha, longing to be freed from restraint, caused his minister to be arrested, when he came the next day to the palace, as usual, unsuspicious of danger. This very day he will be led round the city, be proclaimed a traitor, and have his eyes put out.

"I, having lost my only friend and protector, have no wish to live, and was fastening my sash to hang myself, when you interrupted me."

When Purnabhadra had finished this story, I said to him, "I am that child who was exposed in the cemetery, and saved by the fairy. My coming here is indeed opportune, and with your assistance I will engage to deliver my father. I would boldly attack the guards as they lead him round the city, but fear, lest in the confusion he might be killed, when all my exertions would have been in vain; some other plan must therefore be thought of."

While I was thus speaking to him a serpent put out his head from a hole near me, and, knowing how to charm serpents, I made it come forth, and secured it.

Then I said to Purnabhadra: "O friend, this is just what I wanted. I will mix with the crowd when my father is led round, let this serpent fall on him as if by chance, and then run up to him and say that I am skilled in charms, and can save his life. No doubt they will allow me to try, and I will stop the effect of the poison in such a manner that he will not die, and yet remain insensible, as if dead.

Meanwhile, do you go to my mother, ask to see her in private, and tell her that the son whom she had lost is now here. Explain to her my plan for saving my father, and say that when she hears of the death of her husband, she must go to the king as if in the greatest grief, and ask for permission to burn herself together with the dead body. When this request is granted, as no doubt it will be, she must prepare the funeral pile, and make ready for self-immolation, laying the apparently dead body on a couch in a private room till I come, when I will tell her what is further to be done."

Purnabhadra, delighted with the plan which I proposed, no longer wished to destroy himself. He set out at once to do as I had directed him, and I went immediately into the city. There I saw great crowds already collected, and ascertained where the executioner would stand when the proclamation was made.

Overhanging the place, there happened to be a large tree, with thick foliage. Into this I climbed, and waited patiently, listening to the talk of the people collected underneath.

Presently the executioner and his men came, bringing the prisoner, and the proclamation was made three times.

"Know all men that this traitor, Kāmapāla, has not only poisoned the late king and his eldest son, but has been convicted of plotting against the life of his present majesty; he endeavoured to persuade two of the king's faithful attendants to administer poison, but they have given information, and his life is justly forfeited; the king, however, in consideration of his being a brahman, and nearly connected with himself, has spared his life, and only sentenced him to have his eyes put out. Let all evil-doers take warning by his punishment."

While this proclamation was being read, I climbed to a branch of the tree just over my father, and dropped on him the poisonous serpent, which immediately bit him. In the confusion which ensued, I slipped down from the tree, and, having mixed with the crowd, managed, while shouting out "This is a just punishment from heaven; so may all traitors perish," to get close to my father, and quickly applied a charm in such a manner that, though he fell down apparently dead, the effect of the poison was stopped. The executioner being also bitten; and his assistants, as well as the crowd of spectators, being alarmed and dispersed from dread of the poisonous serpent; this act of mine was not noticed.

Meanwhile, my mother, who had been prepared by Purnabhadra to hear of her husband's death, went immediately to the king, attended by a large number of friends, and said: "The gods know if my husband was your enemy or not; I will not now attempt to defend him; but, whether he was innocent or guilty, your anger should cease now he is dead. I pray you to allow me to burn his body, and according to the custom of widows of my rank, to ascend the funeral pile together with him. Were I not to perform this duty, disgrace would fall on you and on the whole family, as well as on myself."

The king, well pleased to have got rid of the obnoxious minister, without incurring the sin of killing him, exclaimed: "This death is indeed the act of fate!" And, immediately granting her request, permitted the body of Kāmapāla to be taken to his own house, where I had by that time arrived, and was ready to receive it.

Meanwhile, my mother prepared for death, and, resisting all the entreaties of her friends and servants, expressed her determination to be burnt together with her husband.

When everything for the funeral was arranged, she came into the private room, where the body had been laid, and there saw her husband fully recovered, and me sitting by him. Great was her delight and astonishment at this wonderful and sudden change; and having first embraced her husband, she threw her arms round me, and, with a voice broken by sobs of joy, said: "O, my darling son, how can I deserve such happiness?—I, who so cruelly abandoned you at your birth, and suffered you to be taken away, as if dead? but your father was not to blame for that; he, indeed, deserves to have been restored to life by you, and to have the happiness of seeing you. Cruel, indeed, was Tārāvali, who, when she had received you again from Kuvera, did not bring you at once to me; but what could I expect from her? It is through her unkindness in leaving us that all this misfortune has happened; but I must not complain; I was not worthy, without previous suffering, to enjoy such great happiness. Come and embrace me."

Saying this, she again threw her arms round me, and kissed me repeatedly, trembling with emotion, and shedding many tears of joy.

My father's feelings were scarcely less excited. He seemed to have risen from the lowest depth of misery to the summit of felicity, and esteemed himself more fortunate than even Indra the King of the Gods.

When we were all somewhat calmed, and I had explained to my father all that had occurred, I said: "There is much yet to be done; the king will soon find out the deception which has been practised, and send to arrest you again; so we must consider how we can defend ourselves."

My father answered: "This house is a very large one; the walls are strong; there are many secret passages; I have a great store of weapons; my servants are brave and faithful, so that we could hold out for several days. Besides this I have many friends in the city; most of the authorities will favour me; many of the soldiers will be on my side, and there are many persons discontented and ready to rebel against the king. Therefore, if we act prudently, we shall have much assistance, and be able to cut off that tyrant."

With this I entirely agreed, and we prepared for defence. As I had expected, the king, finding how he had been deceived, sent soldiers to take us; but, though they made many attempts, we drove them back day after day, with very small loss to ourselves.

Meanwhile, fearing lest we should at last be overpowered, if something more were not done, I determined, if possible, to seize the person of the king; and, as my father's house was not far from the palace, I began to make an underground passage inside, in order to reach his sleeping-room, the exact position of which I had learnt from my father.

After digging for some distance, I came, to my great astonishment, into a large, lofty, well-lighted room, occupied by a number of women, among whom was a young lady of surpassing beauty, resembling the wife of Kāma, or the tutelary goddess of the city, who had hidden herself here to avoid the sight of so much wickedness above.

The women were equally astonished at seeing me, and ran away, alarmed, into other adjoining rooms. One old woman, however, remained behind, and, falling at my feet, said: "Have pity on us poor helpless women; surely thou art a god, for no mortal could have thus found his way hither. O tell us why thou art come."

"Calm yourself," I answered, "You have nothing to fear from me. I am Arthapāla, the son of the minister Kāmapāla and the

Princess Kantimati, and have come thus unexpectedly on you while making an underground passage from my father's house to the palace; but tell me who you all are, and how you come to be living here."

"O prince," she answered, "I had heard of your birth, but not of your preservation, and happy am I now to see you. Know that the young lady whom you have just seen is the granddaughter of your maternal grandfather, Chandasinha. The eldest son of that king died before his father, leaving his wife pregnant, and she lost her life in giving birth to this daughter, who was committed to my care. One day the king sent for me, and said: 'I intend this child when grown up to be given in marriage to Darpasāra, son of the King of Mālwa; and, remembering the misconduct of her aunt, I am determined that nothing of the kind shall happen with her. I have therefore caused a spacious palace to be made underground, and have furnished it with provisions and all other necessaries for even a hundred years. I have great confidence in you; you will therefore go down into this subterranean dwelling, taking with you the princess and such attendants as you may think desirable, and will remain there until she is grown up, when I shall fetch you from below, and give her in marriage as I have intended.' So saying, he lifted up a small trap-door in the court-yard close to his own apartment, and showed me the steps leading to this place. The next day we all came down, and have remained here ever since. Twelve years have now passed, and the king seems to have forgotten us. I must tell you also that the princess, though destined by her grandfather for Darpasāra, was originally intended for you; for her mother, while the child was as yet unborn, promised that her daughter should become the wife of the son of Kantimati if he should ever return. Look on her, therefore, as your intended, and do what is best for us."

Having received this account from the old woman, I told her to have no fear on the princess's account, but to trust entirely in me, and that I would soon liberate them from their long and tedious imprisonment.

She then took a lamp and showed me the steps leading to the trap-door, which I forced open, and soon found my way into the king's bed-room. There, before he was sufficiently awake to call for help, I seized, gagged, and bound him, and dragging him along, as an ichneumon drags a serpent, past the astonished women and through the tunnel which I had made, I brought him, trembling with fear and bowed down by shame, to my father's house, and showed him to my parents, telling them how I had captured him, and how I had discovered the princess in the subterranean palace.

When the seizure of the king was known, those who were previously well-disposed to my father immediately joined us, and all opposition ceased.

Soon afterwards I married the princess, who looked on me as her deliverer from the dungeon; Sinhaghosha was deposed; and I, having a double claim to the throne, was acknowledged king in his stead.

Hearing that the King of Anga, a devoted friend of your father, was at war, and attacked by a strong enemy, we have marched hither with an army to his assistance, and I have had the pleasure of helping to deliver him from his enemies, and the still greater happiness of meeting with you. I now beg of you to decide what shall be done with the deposed king, our prisoner, whom we have brought with us. My mother is very anxious to liberate him, but hitherto it has not been thought safe to do so.

The prince answered: "Let that unworthy young man be freed, on condition of giving up all claim to the throne and leading a private life; and let him devote himself to pious meditation, which is the purifier of evil deeds." Then turning with a kind look to Pramati, he said: "Do you now relate your adventures," with which request he at once complied:—

ADVENTURES OF PRAMATI.

MY LORD, while wandering like the rest of your friends in search of you, I found myself one evening in a large forest, far from any habitation. Thinking it useless to attempt to go further in an unknown country and in darkness, I prepared to sleep there. Having bathed in the water of a small lake, and made myself a bed of leaves, I lay down under a large tree, commending myself to the deities presiding over the place, and was very soon asleep.

Presently a strange and delightful feeling came over me, gladdening my inmost soul; and I awoke, hardly knowing whether what I saw was a reality or a dream, for on looking round me I saw that I was no longer in the forest, but in a very large and lofty room, lying on a soft couch with white muslin curtains; all around me were a number of sleeping women. Among them my eyes were especially attracted towards a young lady of exceeding beauty, lying in a very graceful attitude, covered only by a silken petticoat, her bosom slowly rising and falling, and her bud-like lower lip quivering with the soft movement of the breath in quiet sleep.

Lost in astonishment, I said to myself: "What has become of that great forest wrapt in darkness? How is my bed of leaves exchanged for this soft couch? Whence is this dome above me, lofty as the great temple of Siva? Who are all these lovely women, like a troop of Apsaras lying down wearied with play? And who can this beautiful lady be? She cannot be a goddess, for the gods do not sleep thus, nor do they perspire, and I see the drops breaking forth on her forehead. She must then be a mortal; but O how lovely! how peacefully she sleeps, as if she had never known the anxieties of love! My heart is drawn towards her."

With these thoughts I rose up and approached the bed where she lay, and stood looking at her as if entranced, becoming every moment more enamoured, longing to touch her, but held back by the fear of disturbing her.

While I was thus gazing, she gradually awoke, and, raising herself into a sitting posture, looked at me attentively with eyes more than half closed. At first her lips were opened, as if she were about to cry out; but, apparently restrained by some secret power, she remained silent, trembling all over, and showing in her countenance the signs of mingled doubt, fear, astonishment, bashfulness, and love; till at last, overcome again by sleep, she slowly sank down again on the bed.

Almost at the same time I felt myself irresistibly overcome by drowsiness, and was very soon fast asleep.

When I awoke, I found myself on the bed of leaves once more, alone in the gloomy forest, and day was beginning to appear.

When I was quite awake I had some difficulty in collecting my thoughts, and I said to myself: "Can all this of which I have such a vivid impression be other than a reality, or was it only a dream, a magical delusion? Whatever it may be, I will not quit this place till I find out the truth, and I will place myself under the protection of the deity who sent the vision."

Having formed this resolution, I was waiting where I had slept, when I saw approaching me a female form faded like a flower scorched by the sun, with eyes red from weeping, lips parched by the hot breath of sighs, wearing a scanty black dress, without ornaments, and with her hair in a single braid, like an affectionate wife mourning for the absence of her husband;* and with all this having an air of divine dignity, which made me regard her with reverence, and think that she might be the tutelary goddess of the place, to whom I had commended myself; and I prostrated myself before her. But she raised me up with

* Hindoo women, when absent from their husbands, always wear, or used to wear, their hair done up into a single braid.

her arms, and after kissing me again and again, said, with a voice broken by tears and sobs, "O, my darling, surely you have heard from the Queen Vasumati how one night a fairy appeared to her, and placing the child Arthapāla* in her arms, told her husband's name and her own; and how the child was brought by order of Kuvera; and then disappeared. I am that fairy—your mother. Bewildered by unreasonable jealousy and anger, I abandoned my husband, your father, Kāmapāla; and for that sin I was cursed by Durga, who condemned me to be possessed by an evil spirit for a year. That year, which seemed to me like a thousand

* The author has here made a mistake which cannot be explained. In the introductory chapter Pramati is the son of Sumati, and there is nowhere mention of a second son of Kāmapāla. The confusion of names is, however, of little importance, since the adventures of Arthapāla and Pramati are quite distinct.

years, is ended; and I am now come from the great festival of Siva, where I have met my relations, who had assembled there, and have received full pardon from the goddess.

"In my way thither, I passed by this place, saw you about to lie down, and heard your prayer to the local deity.

"Being still partly under the influence of the curse, I did not recognise you as my son. Yet even as a stranger I felt an interest in you, and could not bear the thought of leaving you exposed to danger in such a wild place. I therefore waited till you were fast asleep; and having considered where I could deposit you while I was gone to meet the goddess, since I could not take you with me, it occurred to me to carry you to the palace of the King of Sravasti, and leave you to sleep there till my return.

I therefore carried you through the air, and placed you in the sleeping apartment of the Princess Navamālika, feeling sure that no one would disturb you there. I then went to the temple; and after paying due worship to Siva, and receiving the congratulations of my assembled friends, I was dismissed by the goddess, who said: 'You are forgiven; the curse is ended; go and be happy with your husband.' After which I returned to the palace; and taking you up, brought you to this place, and laid you, still sleeping, on your bed of leaves. Since then, I have been watching for your awaking; for as soon as the curse was removed, I knew you to be my son.

"I must now leave you, and go to your father. I know what passed in the palace; how you have fallen in love with the princess, and her feelings towards you. Do not despond; before long you will see her again."

She then warmly embraced me; and saying: "I go with reluctance, farewell for the present," she departed.

Having thus found the supposed dream to be a reality, and that the lady whom I had seen was the Princess Navamālika, I was confirmed in my love, and set out for Sravasti, determined, if possible, to see her again.

On the road, I came to a village where there was a large fair and a great concourse of traders. Various amusements were going on; among others, a cock-fight, which I stopped to look at, and sat down near an old brahman, who was watching the fight with great interest. On seeing me smile, he asked the reason; and I answered: "What simpletons some of the breeders here must be to pit a Balāka cock against one of the Nārikela breed, which is sure to win."

With a knowing look, he whispered to me: "Hush! these blockheads know no better. I see you are a sharp fellow; sit quiet and say nothing." Then he offered me betel and pawn from his box; and we got into conversation.

Meanwhile, the birds fought furiously; and there was much vociferation on both sides; but, as I had predicted, the Balāka cock was beaten. The old man was delighted at the victory of the other, which was his own. He seemed to have taken a great liking to me, though our ages were so different, and invited me to his house, where I was very hospitably treated, and passed the night.

The next morning he accompanied me some distance on the way to Sravasti; and said, at parting: "Remember, I am your friend; do not hesitate to apply to me if there is anything in which I can help you."

After he had left me, I continued my journey; and arriving late and very tired at Sravasti, I lay down to sleep in an arbour in one part of the park outside the city. There I slept soundly till awakened by the noise of the swans and other birds in a lake not far off.

Soon after I had risen, I heard the tinkling of anklets, and saw a young lady walking towards me, with a painted canvas in her hand. When she came near, she looked first at me, and then at the painting. This she did several times, and was evidently surprised and pleased at the comparison

On casting an eye on the picture, I also was much surprised, finding it to be a portrait of myself.

Feeling sure that the likeness could not be accidental, and that there must be some reason for her making the comparison and seeming so pleased at the result, I would not at first make any inquiry of her, but merely said: "This is a public place; we need not stand on ceremony; pray sit down with me." This she did; and we got into conversation about the news of the town.

At last she said to me: "You seem to be quite a stranger here, and look as if you were travel-tired. Will you be offended if I ask you to come and rest at my house?"

"Offended!" I answered. "You do me a very great favour; I shall be most delighted to accept your invitation." Upon this, she rose, and I followed her to her house, where I was most kindly entertained.

When I was refreshed with bathing and food, she said to me: "You have been travelling about in various countries. Have you, in your travels, met with any very extraordinary adventure?"

On hearing this question, I thought: "I have now good ground for hope. The picture represents that very room which I saw, with its lofty ceiling and white canopies—even the bed where the princess was lying. Instigated by love, she has doubtless painted my portrait from recollection; and, in the hope that I may be discovered through the likeness, has entrusted it to this lady who has now invited me to her house. She evidently thinks that I am the person;

but hesitates to put a direct question to me. If I am right, I will soon remove her doubt."

I asked her, therefore: "Will you allow me to examine that picture?" She put it into my hand; and I drew on it the princess lying as I had seen her; and giving it back, said: "One night, while sleeping in a forest, I had a very wonderful dream. I found myself lying in just such a room as that which is represented in this painting; and saw there a very beautiful young lady, such as I have painted here; could that have been anything more than a dream?"

When she heard this, her face lighted up, and she answered: "That was no dream, but a reality; and you are indeed the person I was looking for." Then she told me the whole story; how the princess had seen and fallen in love with me; and how she had painted that picture and given it to her friend, that it might be the means of discovering me; and how delighted she would now be to hear that I was found at last.

I begged her to assure the princess that I was even more anxious to see her, and had come to Sravasti solely from the hope of finding her.

"If your friend is disposed to favour me," I continued, "beg her to wait patiently a few days; I will arrange a plan which will enable us to be together in her apartments, without danger to either of us." To this she agreed, and having taken leave of her, I went back to the village where the old brahman lived, whom I had met at the cock-fight. I found him at home, and delighted to see me. After I was rested and refreshed, he asked me,

"What has brought you back so soon? is there anything in which you require my assistance?"

"There is," I answered, "a very important affair, in which you can materially assist me. The King of the Sravastans, Dharmavardhana,* whose character corresponds with his name, has a very beautiful daughter. By an extraordinary chance, I have seen and fallen in love with her. I have reason to believe that she was equally struck by me, but know not how to contrive a meeting between us without your help; will you therefore assist me?"

"What is your plan?" he asked, "and how can I be of service in carrying it out?"

"My plan is this," I replied. "I will dress as a woman, and pass for your daughter; and

* Increaser of virtue.

you are so clever and ready-witted, that I think you will be able to get me into the palace as a companion to the princess, and even to manage so that she shall become my wife." Then I told him how I thought this might be accomplished; and he quite approved of what I proposed, entered into it with great spirit, and promised his ready co-operation.

Accordingly, the first day that the king was sitting in public to administer justice, the old man approached, followed by me dressed as a woman, walking modestly behind him, and bowing down to the king, he said: "My lord, I have heard of your great beneficence, and how you are the father of all your subjects, the protector and friend of the helpless; I am therefore come to ask a great favour. This girl is my only daughter. Her mother died soon after her birth. I have brought her up, and she has never left me; but I am desirous now to be relieved of this charge and to see her well married. A long time ago, she was engaged to a young brahman, who went to Oujein, to study there, and acquire the means of supporting a wife and family. I have been expecting his return for some time, but have heard nothing of him; I am, therefore, very uneasy on my daughter's account, and purpose to go to Oujein, and find out whether he is alive or dead. I cannot leave my daughter alone, and have no friend or near relation with whom I can place her. Will your majesty deign to allow her to remain under your protection until my return?"

To this the king graciously assented, and I was received into the palace, where I soon found means of letting the princess know of my disguise, and was taken into her apartments as one of her immediate attendants.

Thus our wishes were gratified, and we enjoyed uninterrupted intercourse with each other. But more was yet to be done, and when the time was nearly arrived at which it had been arranged between me and the old brahman that he was to come to fetch me, I said to my darling: "To-morrow, as you know, there will be a procession to a certain holy place near the river; you and your attendants will join in it and have an opportunity of bathing there. While we are in the water, I will scream out, as if drowning, and, diving underneath the surface, will come up among the bushes a long way off, without being seen. Do you appear greatly distressed at my death; but fear nothing, I shall soon come to you again."

Accordingly, the next day, while bathing in the Ganges, I made it appear as if I were accidentally carried out of my depth and drawn in by one of the eddies of the river, and screamed out loudly for help. My cries and screams and subsequent disappearance caused a great commotion, and long search was made for my body; but of course in vain, for I had dived under, and come to the surface unobserved among the thick bushes at the place which had been agreed upon. There, having gone on shore, I soon found the old brahman, who was waiting for me with a suit of men's clothes, and, putting them on, I walked quietly with him into the town.

The next day, as if he had heard nothing of the loss of his pretended daughter, he went to the king, accompanied by me, and said: "My lord, I have returned from Oujein, and have brought with me this young man, the intended husband of my daughter, with whom I am much pleased, and whom I can confidently recommend to your favour, for I have heard an exceedingly good report of him there. He is not only very learned in the vedas and commentaries, advanced in science and arts, well instructed in politics and history, clever in reciting stories and poetry, but is a bold and skilful rider, a good archer and swordsman. There is scarcely anything that a young man should know, with which he is not familiar; and, with all this, he is free from conceit, good-tempered, gentle, and kind; in short, he seems to me almost perfect, and more fit to marry a princess than the daughter of such a man as I am. When I have seen my child happily married to him, I shall not trouble them with my society, but withdraw from the world, and end my days in a hermitage. I have now come to take back my daughter, with the most humble and heartfelt gratitude for the gracious protection which you have so kindly afforded her." With these words he bowed himself to the ground in humble obeisance.

On hearing this the king was greatly perplexed, and obliged to admit that the girl had been drowned while bathing, and that her body had not been found.

Then the old man began to tear his hair, beat his breast, and show signs of the most extravagant grief, calling on the king to restore his dear daughter, and reproaching him with having caused her death. In vain did the king make him large offers of compensation; he refused them all, declaring it to be his firm intention to put himself to death at the gate of the palace, and so cause the sin to fall on the king's head.*

He, despairing of finding any other way of appeasing the old man, after some consideration and consultation with his ministers, said to him: "You have told me that your intended son-in-law is a young man of rare abilities, and more fit to be the husband of a princess than of your daughter, and his appearance is very prepossessing; I offer him then my daughter in the place of yours. Will this satisfy you?" Then at last the old man professed to be contented; I was treated with much honour, in due time became the husband of the princess, and reached the summit of my wishes.

After a time, an army was sent by my

* It was considered a very great sin to be, even indirectly, the cause of the death of a brahman.

father-in-law to the assistance of the King of Anga, and, thinking of the possibility of meeting you here, I solicited and obtained the command of it, and my hopes have been fulfilled, since I have now the great pleasure of seeing you.

Having heard this story, the prince remarked; "You have done no deeds of blood, but have gained your ends by gentleness and ingenuity. This is the way approved of by the wise." Then turning to Mitragupta, he said: "It is now your turn," and he immediately began his story thus:—

ADVENTURES OF MITRAGUPTA.

MY LORD, I set out on my travels in search of you, like the rest, and arriving one day at Damalipta, I saw a great crowd collected in a large park outside the city. While looking about me to find some one of whom I might inquire what this festival was, I espied a young man, sitting alone in an arbour, amusing himself with playing on a lute. Going up to him, I asked: "What is this concourse of people? Why do you sit here alone, away from the others?"

He answered: "A long time ago, the king of this country, having no children, made many prayers and offerings to the goddess

Durga, in the hope of propitiating her. At last she appeared to him in a dream, and said: 'Your prayer is granted; your wife shall bear twins—a daughter who must be your successor, and a son who must be subject to her and to her husband when she marries. Further, it is my will and pleasure that, beginning from her seventh year, you shall make, every month when the moon is in the constellation Krittika (or the Pleiades), a great festival, to be called the Festival of the Ball Dance, at which she shall publicly exhibit her skill before the people. I also will, that in reference to a husband, she shall have free choice without any pressure on your part, and that he whom she marries shall have equal power with her, and reign after your death.'

"The promise given in the dream was fulfilled. The queen bore twins—a son and a daughter. The king has duly obeyed the commands of the goddess, and to-day the princess, whose name is Kandukavati, will again perform the ball dance for the propitiation of Durga in the sight of the people here assembled.

"You asked me also why I am sitting here alone. I will tell you. The Princess Kandukavati has a dear friend and foster-sister, who is engaged to me.

"Of late, Bhímadhanwa, the brother of the princess, has cast his eyes on her, and persecuted her with his importunities. Knowing his character, I have great fear lest some day he should use violence towards her. This is why I am so anxious and uneasy, and have no inclination to join in the festivities."

Just then I heard the tinkling of anklets,

and a young lady came to the place where we were sitting.

On seeing her, my companion started up with great delight, and, taking her by the hand, introduced her to me, saying: "This is the lady whom I have told you of, dearer to me than life, the thought of separation from whom, through the wickedness of that wretch, burns me like fire, and causes me to suffer misery greater than death. I have no loyalty or respect towards him, and will lose my life rather than suffer him to accomplish his wicked purpose."

But she, with tears in her eyes, said: "O my beloved, do not on my account engage in any act of violence; whatever might be the result, your own life would certainly be forfeited. You have continually professed your great love for me; be guided now by my advice. I am ready to follow you wherever you go; let us then fly from this country, and go where we shall be safe from my persecutor."

My new acquaintance then turned to me, and said: "You seem to have been a great traveller; tell us in what country we may be most in safety and best able to live."

I smiled at this, and answered: "The world is wide, and there are plenty of countries pleasant to live in; but, after all, one's own country is the best; why should you banish yourselves? I think I can contrive some means by which you will be enabled to remain here in safety and comfort. Wait then a while, and if I cannot do this I will tell you where it will be best for you to go."

Before we had time to say more, the young girl started up, saying: "I dare not stay a moment longer. I have stopped away from my mistress to see you, and now I hear her coming, and must join her directly. Any one may see the princess at this festival; I hope you will have a good view of her." Saying this to me, she ran off, and we both followed her to the place where the princess was to perform — an open stage which had been erected in the park.

Presently she made her appearance, followed by a train of female attendants, and the moment I saw her my heart was drawn towards her. I almost doubted whether she were a goddess or a mortal; but when she began to play, I was even more captivated by her graceful movements than I had been by her beauty.

First she made a low obeisance in honour of the goddess; then taking up the bright red ball with her slender fingers, she let it drop as if accidentally, and striking it as it rebounded, caught it on the back of her hand and sent it high into the air; then she made it rise and fall, at first slowly, then faster, and then very rapidly, keeping time to it by graceful movements of the feet. Sometimes it seemed to stand still, sometimes to fly up like a bird; at one time she would strike it alternately with her right hand and left hand; at another send it high into the air, dancing meanwhile to her own singing; then the ball would go quite away, and come back as if of itself. Thus she went on a long time amidst the applause of the surrounding spectators, performing various graceful movements, striking the ball with feet as well as hands, and even making it whirl round and round her so rapidly that she seemed to be enclosed in a fiery red cage; now with one hand holding up her dress or replacing her hair which had fallen down, and keeping the ball in motion with the other; now taking several balls and keeping them all in the air at once.

At last the performance was ended; and, after again making a low obeisance in honour of the goddess, she walked slowly round the stage, leaning on the arm of her foster-sister Chandrasena, and followed by her maidens, casting several significant glances at me, and especially giving me one long lingering look as she withdrew.

My new friend, Kosadāsa, who had stood near me all the time, invited me to his house, where I was most hospitably entertained.

In the evening, Chandrasena, the lady to whom he had introduced me, came to see him.

I said to her: "I promised to find some means of freeing you from the importunities of the prince; this is what I have thought of. I have a magic ointment, a small quantity of which applied to your face will make you look like a monkey in the eyes of all who see you. Your persecutor will certainly then be disgusted, and give you no more annoyance."

"Truly I am exceedingly obliged to you," she answered, "for such a charming proposal. But whatever I may be in a future birth, I have no inclination to be turned into a monkey now. If you have nothing better than this to propose, we shall not esteem your wisdom very highly. Happily, I have thought of something much better. You have heard that, according to the word of Durga, the princess is to be allowed free choice of a husband. You are greatly in love with her, and she is favourably disposed towards you, from your appearance. My mother, of whom she is very fond, will do everything in her power to promote your interests; and no doubt she will choose you. The king and queen will of course give their consent; and the marriage once completed, there will be no further danger, since Bhímadhanwa will be subject to you, and you will be able easily to protect me. Wait, therefore, a few days, and I and my mother will do our best on your behalf. But I must not stay longer; my mistress will be waiting for me."

After she was gone, Kosadāsa and I got into conversation about that which so greatly concerned us both; and so much interested were we, that we never thought of going to bed, but sat up talking all the night.

In the morning, I went to the park, and stood for some time near the stage on which I had seen the princess; and in imagination saw her there again, in some of those graceful attitudes which she had displayed. While I was thus deep in thought, I was accosted by Bhímadhanwa, who introduced himself to me, appeared very friendly, sat down with me, and, after some conversation, invited me to his house.

Having no suspicion of treachery, I accompanied him to the palace, where I was most hospitably entertained. After dinner, not having slept the night before, I lay down, and was soon fast asleep, and dreaming of my beloved princess. Presently, I was suddenly awakened, and found my arms bound with an iron chain, and Bhimadhanwa, with angry countenance, standing near me.

"Vile wretch!" he said. "You fancied you could plot in safety; and little thought that all which that girl said was overheard, and brought to me by one of my spies, who heard it through the open window. My silly sister, forsooth, is in love with you! You are to marry her, and make me your subject; and you will order me to give up Chandrasena, that she may marry her lover! You are much mistaken. I am not so easily managed as that. We shall soon see how all your fine projects will end." Then calling two strong men, his servants, at his command they lifted me up, carried me down to the sea, and threw me in as I was.

Notwithstanding the chain which confined my arms, I managed to keep afloat, till by a lucky chance I fell in with a piece of wood, and by throwing myself across it, managed to hold on, and was carried out to sea. After floating all night, in the morning I was seen from a ship sailing that way, and taken on board.

The captain, however, who was a foreigner, had not much compassion on me; and only thought, as I was young and strong, how much he could get by selling me as a slave; and did not even release my hands. I had not been long on board, however, when the ship was attacked by pirates, who surrounded it with their boats, and poured in a shower of arrows and other missiles.

Seeing that the crew of the merchant-ship were being defeated, I called out to the captain: "Take off my chain; set me free; and I will soon drive away the enemy."

He did as I asked; and furnished me with a good bow and arrows, which I used so effectually, that a large number of the enemy were killed or wounded; and the boats began to draw off.

Meanwhile, our ship had drifted close to the pirates' galley. I leapt on board, and most of the crew being disabled, took prisoner the captain, who turned out to be Bhímadhanwa, the very man who had so treacherously ill-used me. He was utterly astonished at seeing me; and hung down his head ashamed, unable to answer a word, when I said to him: "Where are all your threats and boastings? You are now as completely in my power as I was in yours."

Then the sailors, shouting for joy at the victory, bound him with the chain with which I had been confined; and after taking possession of the pirate ship, we continued the voyage; but being driven out of our course by a contrary wind, landed on an uninhabited island, to get water and wild fruits, and attend to the wounded.

The merchant-captain and crew, delighted at my bravery, and the timely assistance I had rendered them, treated me with the greatest respect. While they were engaged, I walked about to explore the island; and came to a large quantity of stones which had fallen from a high rock. These I crossed over, and going round to the other side, found a gentle slope, covered with trees and flowers. Walking slowly among them, admiring the beautiful scenery and enjoying the cool shade, I arrived, almost imperceptibly and without fatigue, at the summit, where I found a small lake, surrounded with ruby-coloured, variegated rocks, and partly covered with bright lotuses. In this I bathed, and pulled up some of the lotus-plants, the young shoots of which were unusually sweet and good.

As I came out of the water, carrying a large root on my shoulder, I saw standing on the bank a terrible Rakshas in human form, who called out, in an angry tone: "Who are are you? Where do you come from? What are you doing here, destroying my flowers?"

Without showing any sign of fear, I walked boldly up to him, and said: "I am a brahman, who has just escaped many dangers. I was treacherously thrown into the sea, rescued by a merchant-ship, then attacked by pirates; and now, after conquering them, we have put into this island for water. I have much enjoyed my bathe, and wish you good morning."

"Stop!" said he. "You will not get off so easily. You seem a bold fellow, however, and I will give you a chance for life. I shall ask you four questions. If you can answer them, you are free; if not, I shall devour you immediately."

"Very good," I answered; "I am ready to hear them." Then he began:

"What is cruel?"

"A wicked woman's heart."

"What is most to the advantage of a householder?"

"Good qualities in a wife."

"What is love?"

"Imagination."

"What best accomplishes difficult things?"

"Cunning. Dhumini, Gomini, Ratnavati, and Nitambavati," I added, "are examples of what I have said."

"Tell me," said he, "who they were, and how they prove the truth of your answers?"

"Certainly," I replied; "you shall judge for yourself.

"There were formerly in the country of Trigarta three brothers, all wealthy, having several wives, many servants and slaves, and numerous flocks and herds. In their time it happened that there was a great drought; no rain fell for several years; the streams and fountains ceased to flow; the pools and lakes were turned to mud, the beds of rivers almost dry, plants burned up, trees withered; all mirth and festivity were at an end; bands of thieves roamed about; the dead lay unburied or unburnt, and their bodies were scattered over the fields. At last the famine was so great that men began to devour each other. The three brothers, from their great wealth, were able to hold out a long time; but when their stores of corn and rice were all consumed, and their cattle all slaughtered, they, like the rest, were driven to cannibalism. First they killed and ate their slaves; then, even their wives and children, till all were gone but themselves and their three favourite wives. The famine still continuing, they were driven to eat them also, and drew lots which should be killed first. The lot fell on Dhumini, the wife of the youngest brother, who, unable to bear the thought of devouring her, escaped with her in the night. After walking a long way, till they were quite exhausted, they came to a large forest, where they found a well of water, and many fruits and roots, besides deer and other animals, on which they were able to live without difficulty; and they built a hut there.

"One day when the husband of Dhumini was going about in search of game, he found a man who had been cruelly treated by robbers; they had cut off his hands, feet, and nose, and left him to perish. Having compassion on the poor wretch, he bound up his wounds as well as he was able, and carried him with much difficulty to his hut. There he and his wife nursed him till his wounds were healed, and took care of him afterwards.

"Now such is the depravity of women, that Dhumini fell in love with this poor mutilated wretch, and determined to have him whether he would or no.

"One day her husband came home from hunting, tired and thirsty, and asked her for water. She answered: 'I have a very bad headache, you must go and draw for yourself.' Then walking softly behind him as he went, she waited till he stooped down over the well, and pushed him in.

"Having thus, as she thought, got rid of her husband, she took the maimed man on her back and carried him till she reached an inhabited country, where there was no famine, telling those who asked her, that this man was her husband, and had been mutilated in that manner by a spiteful enemy.

"She thus became the object of much compassion, and praise, for devotion to her husband, and the king of the country bestowed on her a small pension on which she lived in the city of Avanti. Meanwhile her real husband had managed to climb up from the well, and wandered about a long time, not knowing where his wife was gone. At last he came to Avanti in great distress, and was begging for food when she chanced to see him. Going at once to the king, she said, 'That wicked wretch who mutilated my husband is now here; I have seen him going about as a beggar.'

"Upon this he was immediately seized, and, notwithstanding his protestations of innocence, condemned to death, and led away to execution.

"On the way, with but faint hopes of saving his life, he said to the executioner, 'I have been condemned on the evidence of one witness only; let that man whom I am accused of injuring be questioned; if he says I am guilty, then indeed I deserve to die.'

"The executioner saying, 'Perhaps he may be innocent—a few minutes' delay can do no harm,' took him at once to the house of his wife, and there the poor mutilated wretch, with many tears, declared the kindness with which he had been treated by the supposed criminal, and the wickedness of the woman who had forced him to live with her as her husband.

"Thereupon the execution was stayed, and the king, having been made acquainted with the whole affair, ordered her to be cut in pieces and given to the dogs, and showed much favour and kindness to her husband.

"I say, therefore, there is nothing so cruel as the heart of a wicked woman."

The Rakshas appeared to be satisfied with this story, and said: "Go on, tell me about Gomini." I continued therefore:

"There was formerly in the country of the Dravidas a young brahman of great wealth. Somehow he was not married when a mere boy, as is often the case, and when he grew up he thought to himself: 'Those who have no wives and those who have bad wives are equally unfortunate, I will not let my friends choose for me, but travel about and look out for myself till I find a girl who may suit me.'

"Having formed this resolution, and changed his name, he set out alone, taking very little with him, but a small bag containing two or three pounds of rice in the husk.

"Whenever he saw a maiden of his own caste whose appearance he liked, either in the houses where he was admitted or elsewhere, he would say to her: 'My dear, could you make me a good dinner with this rice?' This he did many times, but though parents in general would have been willing to give him their daughters, he was always laughed at, and often treated with contempt.

"One day, while sitting in a public place in a town which he had lately entered, he observed a young girl whose parents had fallen into poverty, which was shown by her scanty dress and slender ornaments. She passed by him accompanied by an old woman, and stood for a time very near him.

"The more he looked at her the more he was pleased, and thought to himself: 'This is just the wife to suit me; she is neither too tall nor too short, too stout or too thin; her limbs are rounded and well knit; her back is straight, with a slight hollow; her shoulders are low; her arms plump and soft; the lines of her hands indicate good fortune; her fingers are long and slender; her nails are like polished gems; her neck is smooth and rounded as a slender shell; her bosom full and well shaped; her face has a sweet expression; her lips are full and red; her chin small and compact; her cheeks plump; her eyebrows glossy black, gracefully curved, meeting in the middle; her eyes are long and languishing, very black and very white; her forehead, adorned by beautiful curls, resembles a piece of the moon; her ears are delicately formed, and well set off by the ear-rings; her hair is glossy black, brown at the ends—long, thick, and not too much curled. My heart seems to be drawn towards her; if she is what she seems to be, I will certainly marry her; but I must not act rashly; I will first try her with my test. Then approaching her with a polite salutation, he said: 'My dear, are you clever enough to make a good dinner out of this bag of rice?' Without answering a word, she looked significantly at her old nurse, and taking the rice from his hand, signed him to sit down on a terrace close by, and sat down herself near him. Then, first spreading out the rice in the sun that it might be quite dry, she rubbed it gently between her hands, so as to get off the husk unbroken, and giving it to the nurse, she said: 'Take this to some goldsmith; they use it when prepared in this way for polishing their gold, and you will get a few pence for it —with them buy a little firewood, a few cheap dishes, and an earthen pipkin, and bring also a wooden mortar with a long pestle.' On this errand the old woman departed, and soon returned, bringing the things required.

"Then the girl put the rice into the mortar, and very gracefully moving the pestle up and down, separated the rice thoroughly from the remaining particles of husk and awns, which she carefully winnowed away.

"After this she washed the rice thoroughly,

and the old woman having meanwhile lighted a fire and placed the pipkin full of water on it, she threw the rice into the water as soon as it boiled, in such a manner that the grains lay loose and separate. When they began to swell and burst, she took the pot from the fire, which she raked together, and set it with the lid downwards near the embers, first carefully draining off the rice liquor, and stirring the grains several times with a spoon to prevent their sticking together.

"After this she put out the fire by throwing water on it, and taking the charcoal, sent the old woman to sell it, and with the money to procure some herbs, ghee, curds, tamarind fruit, spices, salt, myrobalan, and sesamum oil. When these things were brought, she mixed the myrobalan, finely pounded, with salt, and desired the nurse to give it with the sesamum oil to the young brahman, and tell him to go and bathe and anoint himself; and he having received these things, went to bathe.

"When he was returned and comfortably seated, she gave him to drink rice liquor, mixed with spices and cooled by fanning, and he was much refreshed by it; afterwards, soup made with some of the liquor, a few spoonfuls of rice, butter, and spices; and, lastly, the rest of the rice mixed with curds, buttermilk, and several condiments, and he had plenty, though some was left.

"When he had finished, he asked for drink. She gave him water in a new cooler, sweetened and perfumed with lotus and other flowers; and it looked and felt so cool, gurgled so pleasantly, and tasted so sweet, that all his senses were gratified, and he drank eagerly again and again.

"After waiting on him in this manner, as soon as the dishes and the remains of the meal had been removed by the old nurse, she sat down beside him, arranging her scanty patched dress as well as she was able.

"The young brahman having thus satisfied himself of the capabilities of the maiden, made known his real name and position to her parents, and they having gladly accepted him, he married the girl in due form, and took her home to his own house.

"Not very long afterwards, with very little consideration for her, he took to himself another wife, a woman of bad character; yet such was the sweetness of temper of the first, that she showed no anger at this, but continued to treat her husband with all due honour and respect, and so gained over her fellow-wife that she became her dearest friend. At the same time she managed the household admirably, keeping everything in order, yet making all the servants attached to her. In short, she acted in such a manner that she entirely gained the respect and affection of her husband, and he enjoyed great happiness, and trusted and consulted her in all affairs.

"Therefore I say that the best thing for a householder is to have a good wife."

Then, in illustration of the third answer, I related the story of Ratnavati. "There was, in a town in the country of Surat, a rich ship-captain who had a daughter named Ratnavati. She was married to Balabhadra, the son of a merchant living in another town. For some reason he took a sudden dislike to his bride on the very day of the wedding, and though she continued to live in his house, avoided her as much as possible, and would never speak to her, notwithstanding the remonstrances of his friends. The rest of the family and the servants, seeing this, treated her with neglect and contempt, so that she led a most wretched life.

"One day, wandering about disconsolate, she met with an old woman, a buddhist mendicant, who, seeing her weeping and looking miserable, asked her the reason. She, thinking that this woman might possibly be possessed of some charm capable of bringing back her husband's affections, half unwillingly told her the cause of her grief.

"'On the very day of our marriage my husband, from some cause or other, took a sudden dislike to me, and since then he has treated me with neglect and contempt, so that I hardly ever see his face, and then only by chance for a moment, for he avoids me as much as possible; his family also, following his example, behave to me with great unkindness. I have no comfort or happiness, and only wish for death. But you must not tell this to any one; I would not on any account have my misfortune talked about.'

"The old woman answered: 'Surely this must be a punishment for some great sin committed in a former existence, or such a charming person as yourself would never be thus treated by your husband. I recommend you to practise penance and prayer; perhaps the gods may be appeased, and a favourable change produced. Meanwhile, if there is any way in which I can help you, I will gladly do so. You seem very intelligent; cannot you think of some stratagem which may have the desired effect?'

"After reflecting for some time, she said: 'Though my husband so neglects me, I know that he is very fond of women in general, and ready to be captivated by any one, especially a respectable woman who will give him a little encouragement. Acting on this propensity, I think, with your help, that something may be done. There is a young lady, a neighbour, the daughter of a very rich man, in great favour with the Rajah; she is a friend of mine, and is very like me. As my husband hardly knows her by sight, and scarcely ever sees me, it might be possible to pass myself off for her. Do you, therefore, go to him and say that that young lady is in love with him, and that you will introduce him to her, only he must not give a hint that you have told him anything. Meanwhile I will arrange with my friend, and will be walking in her father's garden some evening, when you can bring him in.' The old woman was delighted with this contrivance, and promised to perform her part. She went, therefore, soon afterwards with a pretended message of love from the merchant's daughter to Balabhadra, who was delighted at having attracted the attention of such a charming young lady, and took care to be at the appointed time in the garden, where he saw his neglected wife playing at ball. As if by accident, she threw the ball towards him, and the old woman said: 'This is an invitation; pick up the ball, and take it to her with a pretty speech, and you will get acquainted with her.' In this way an intimacy began, and he often met his wife in the same place in the evening without in the least suspecting the deception. At last she gave him a hint that she was ready to run away with him. Madly in love, he eagerly caught at the proposal, and one night, having collected what money he could carry, he eloped with her, saying nothing to any of his friends. They were much astonished by his sudden disappearance; but when they found that Ratnavati was gone also, they readily believed the story told by the old woman, that he had fallen in love with his own wife, but was ashamed to acknowledge this after having so long neglected her, and was therefore gone to live in another place, where he was not known. Believing this story, her relations and his thought it best to take no steps in the matter, and abstained from making inquiry after him.

"Meanwhile Balabhadra went to a town at some distance, and there by his skill and energy, though beginning with a small capital, amassed in a few years a considerable fortune, and was much respected in the place.

"When Ratnavati eloped under another name, she engaged a woman to accompany her as a servant; and this woman one day having committed some fault, was beaten by her master, who scolded her and told her she was lazy, thievish, and impudent. Smarting under the punishment, she determined to be revenged, and going to the magistrate told him: 'This man, who seems to you so respectable, is a wicked wretch who has abandoned his own wife, and run away in the night with the daughter of one of his neighbours, with whom he is now living.'

"The magistrate having heard this, and being very covetous, thought: 'If this man is convicted, his property will be confiscated, and I shall get a share of it.' He therefore began to take proceedings against Balabhadra, who was greatly alarmed. But his wife said to him, 'Do not be frightened; put a good face on the matter, and say: "This is not Kanakavati, the daughter of Niddhipatidatta; this is my own lawful wife, the daughter of Grihagupta, who lives at Valabhi. She was married to me with the proper ceremony and with the full consent of her parents. This woman's accusation is altogether false; but if you will not believe my assertion, send to Valabhi, to my wife's father, and hear what he will say—or send to the town where I formerly lived, and make inquiries there.'

"This was done, he was admitted to bail, and a letter was written to the father of Ratnavati, who answered it in person, and declared that the lady in question was really his daughter. Thus the matter was settled; but the husband, thinking that the old man was deceived by the likeness, held to his former belief, and continued to live happily with his wife, without ever discovering the delusion. Therefore I say that love is only imagination."

The Rakshas, though appearing to be satisfied with these stories, required me to relate that of Nitambavati, which I proceeded to do.

"In a city called Madhura, there dwelt a man named Kalahakantaka, of great strength and vigour, ready at any time to take up the quarrel of a friend, famed for deeds of violence, and devoted to pleasures and amusements.

"One day he saw a picture exhibited by a painter, a new-comer, and stopped to look at it. It was the portrait of a lady so beautiful that he fell in love with her at once. Desirous of finding out whom it represented, he praised the picture exceedingly, and having put the artist in good humour, got him to say who the lady was. 'Her name,' said he, 'is Nitambavati; she is the wife of a merchant living at Avanti or Oujein, and I was so struck by her beauty that I sought and obtained permission to paint her portrait.'

"On hearing this, Kalahakantaka, taking another name, went to Oujein; and there, having disguised himself as a mendicant, got admission to the merchant's house, saw the lady, whose beauty exceeded even his expectation, and was confirmed in his wicked purpose.

"At this time a guardian or watchman was wanted for the public cemetery, and he applied for and obtained the office.

"With the clothes which he took from the bodies brought to be burnt there, he bribed an old woman to take a message from him. She went to Nitambavati, and said: 'A very handsome young man is much in love with you—pray let him see you if only for once.' On receiving this message, the merchant's wife was very indignant, and sent the old woman away with angry words. Kalahakantaka, however, was not discouraged, and said to his messenger: 'Go again, and say to the lady: "Do you imagine that a person like me, devoted to religious meditation, who have passed so many years in pilgrimages to holy places, would wish to lead you into sin? Far from it. I had heard that you were childless, and wishing for children, and I know of means through which your wish may be accomplished; but I thought it right to find out first whether you were worthy of such a service, and now that I have ascertained you to be virtuous and true to your husband, I will gladly assist you."'

"With this story the old cheat went again to the lady, who, believing her to be sincere, gladly accepted the offer, and she went on to say: 'The reason of your being childless is that a spell has been laid upon your husband, which can only be removed by the means which I will indicate to you. You must go at night to a clump of trees in the park. I will come to you there, and will bring with me a man skilled in incantations. You have only to stand for a moment, putting your foot into his hand while he utters certain charms, then go home, and, as if in play, strike your husband on the breast. This will dissolve the spell, and by-and-by you will have children.'

"Anxious to have the spell removed from her husband, Nitambavati consented to this, and went at night to the appointed place. There she found Kalahakantaka waiting, and as the old woman had directed, put her foot into his hand while he knelt before her.

"No sooner had he got hold of it than he took off her anklet, and slipping his hand up her leg, inflicted a slight wound above the knee, and ran away.

"The poor lady, dreadfully frightened, blaming herself, and enraged with the old woman, who had so cruelly deceived her, got home as well as she could, washed and bound up the cut, and kept her bed for several days, having taken off the other anklet, that the less might not be observed.

"Meanwhile the rascal took the anklet he

had stolen to the husband, saying: 'I wish to dispose of this, will you buy it?'

"Recognising the ornament as having been his wife's, he asked: 'Where did you get this?'

"The man answered: 'I will not tell you now, but if you are not satisfied that it is honestly mine, take me before the magistrates, and I will then declare how I came by it.'

"Upon this the merchant went to his wife and said: 'Let me see your anklets.'

"With some confusion and alarm, she answered: 'I have only one of them, the other being, as I suppose, loosely fastened, dropped off a few days ago when I was walking in the evening in the garden, and I have not been able to find it.'

"Dissatisfied with this answer, the husband

went before the magistrates with the man who had offered the anklet for sale, and he being there questioned, said: 'You know I was appointed not long ago to the care of the public cemetery, and as people come sometimes after dark to steal the clothes, or to lay a dead body on a pile prepared for another, and so cheat me of my fees, I have lately kept watch there at night.'

"'A short time ago I saw a woman in a dark dress dragging away part of a half-burnt body, and ran to seize her. In the struggle her anklet came off, and I gave her a slight wound on the leg, but she got away, and I could not overtake her; this is how the ornament came into my possession. I leave it to you to say whether I have done wrong or no.'

"Then the magistrates and citizens who

were assembled were unanimously of opinion that the woman was a Sākiní.* She was therefore divorced from her husband, and condemned to be tied to a stake in the cemetery, and left there.

"In this state she was found by Kalaha-kantaka, who cut the cords which fastened her, and, falling at her feet, confessed all that he had done, alleging his great love for her as an excuse for his cruel conduct: 'And now,' said he, 'consent to be my wife, and I will carry you away to my own home in a distant country, where you will not be known. I will do everything in my power to make your life happy, and atone for the suffering which I have caused you.'

* An evil spirit, the ghoul of the "Arabian Nights," the readers of which will remember the story of Amina, who goes out at night to feast on dead bodies.

"For a long time the unhappy lady refused; but at last, overcome by his earnest entreaties, and feeling how unjustly she had been disgraced and ill-treated, she consented to accompany him. Thus, by cunning, he gained his end, which he could not have accomplished by any other means. Therefore I say cunning best accomplishes difficult things."

Having heard these stories, the Rakshas was much pleased, and offered me his assistance if I should require it. At that moment several pearls fell close beside us. Looking up to see whence they came, I perceived a Rakshas flying through the air, carrying a woman who was struggling with him.

"Shall that monster carry off the lady before our eyes? O that I could fly to rescue her!"

As I exclaimed thus, my new ally, without waiting to be entreated, sprang into the air, and calling out "Stop! stop! wicked wretch!" attacked and dragged down the other Rakshas. He, in defending himself, when only a short distance from the ground, let the lady fall, and I caught her with outstretched arms in such a manner that, though much shaken and alarmed, she was not seriously injured. I held her for a moment insensible in my arms, while I gazed at the combatants. Their flight was of short duration, for they attacked each other so furiously that both were killed.

Then laying my burden on the soft grass in a shady place, and sprinkling her with water, I soon had the happiness of seeing her open her eyes, and of recognising the beloved of my heart, the Princess Kandukavati, who was equally delighted on finding who was her deliverer.

When sufficiently recovered, she said to me: "On returning home after the ball dance, longing to see you, and sad with the thought that we might never meet again, I was filled with great happiness by the report which Chandrasena brought me of your love; but when I heard that you had been bound and thrown into the sea by my wicked brother, I fell into the deepest despair, and wished for death. Wandering in this state of mind about the gardens, I was espied by that vile Rakshas, who, having assumed a human form, first made love to me, and then, when rejected, forcibly carried me off. He is, happily, now dead, and all that I have suffered is as nothing now that I am with you; let us return as soon as possible to my parents, who will have been greatly distressed at my disappearance."

Without delay I carried her down to the shore, embarked, set sail at once, and the wind being favourable, we soon reached Damalipta. Here we found great confusion and grief among the people, and were told on inquiring: "The king and queen, utterly broken down by the loss of their son and daughter, have determined to abandon life, and have just set out for a holy place on the bank of the Ganges, with the intention of fasting to death there; and several of the old citizens have accompanied them with the same purpose."

On hearing this I immediately went after them, and having soon overtaken them, was able to give them great happiness, by telling them of all that had occurred, and how both their son and daughter were safely returned; and they went back with me to the city, to the great joy of the people. The king treated me with great honour, and not long afterwards the princess became my wife. Her brother was reconciled to me, and at my request, though very reluctantly, gave up all further attention to Chandrasena, who was happily united with her lover.

When King Sinhavarma was attacked as you know, I marched with an army to his assistance, and have thus the great pleasure of meeting with you.

The prince having heard this story said: "Your adventures have indeed been strange, and your escape from death wonderful. Great is the power of fate, but excellent also is courage and presence of mind such as you have shown." Then turning to Mantragupta, he desired him to relate his adventures, which he immediately began to do:—

ADVENTURES OF MANTRAGUPTA.

MY LORD, I also, in my anxiety to find you, wandered about like the others. Late one evening I came to a wood, a few miles from the city of Kalinga, and very near a public cemetery. Seeing no dwelling near, I made myself a bed of leaves, and lay down under a large tree, where I was soon asleep. About midnight, when evil spirits are wont to roam, and everything was quiet around me, I awoke, and fancied I heard a whispering conversation going on among the branches of the tree immediately above me. Listening very attentively, I was able to distinguish these words :

"We are powerless to resist that vile Siddha whenever he chooses to command us; could not some person be found powerful enough to counteract the designs of that vile magician?"

After this the voices ceased, and I thought I could hear a rustling among the branches as if the speakers were moving from tree to tree. This strange occurrence greatly excited my curiosity. I said to myself: "Who are these creatures whose voices I have heard? who can that magician be, and what dreadful thing is it which he is about to do?" With these thoughts, I determined if possible to discover the mystery, and followed, as well as I was able, the direction which the demons, or whatever they were whom I had heard conversing, had taken. Guided by the rustling sound which I still heard above me, I made my way through the darkness, till at last I thought I saw a light in the distance, and going a little further, I perceived a fire shining through the thick foliage. Approaching very cautiously, I saw a Siddha standing near it, his head covered with a large mass of tangled hair, his body begrimed with the dust of charcoal, and a girdle of human bones round his waist. He was throwing at intervals handfuls of sesamum and mustard-seed into the fire, causing flickering flames to rise up and dispel the surrounding darkness. Before him, in humble attitude, stood two Rakshas, male and female, whom I supposed to be those whose voices I had heard in the tree. They said to him, "We await your commands. What are we now to do?"

"Go," he answered in a stern voice,

"immediately to the palace of the King of Kalinga, and bring here his daughter Kanakalekha." This they did in an incredibly short time. As soon as she was brought he seized her by the hair, and disregarding her tears and entreaties and screams for help, was about to cut off her head with a sword.

Meanwhile I had cautiously crept nearer, and perceiving the danger of the princess, I made a sudden rush at him, snatched the sword from his hand and cut off his head.

Seeing this, the two Rakshas approached me, and showing great delight at the death of their cruel master, said to me: "That wicked man has for a long time had power over us; we have continually been compelled to go on his vile errands, and have had no rest night or day. You have done a truly good deed in killing him; your valour has freed us from this slavery; he is gone to the kingdom of Yama, where he will receive the reward of his evil deeds, and we are ready to serve you; say only what is to be done."

I thanked them for their grateful offer, and said: "I have only done what every good man would have done under the circumstances; but if you are willing to serve me, all that I require of you is to carry this lady again to her father's house, from which she was so cruelly taken."

The princess hearing this, stood for a moment irresolute, with her head bent down, her eyes half closed, her eyebrows quivering, her bosom agitated by hurried breathing and wetted by tears of joy, restlessly moving one foot, as if scratching the ground, and betraying the struggle between bashfulness and love by alternate blushes and paleness.

Then, in a low sweet gentle voice, she uttered these words: "O gracious, sir why do you, having just delivered me from a terrible death, now overwhelm me in a sea of love whose waves are the agitations of anxiety driven by the wind of passion? My life, saved by you, is entirely at your disposal. Take pity on me; regard me as your own. Let me be your servant, your slave; I would endure anything rather than separation from you. Come with me to my father's palace; you need not fear discovery; all my friends and attendants are faithful and devoted to me; they will carefully keep the secret."

Pierced to the heart by the arrows of Kama, tied and bound by her looks and words as if with chains of iron, I had no power to refuse, and turning to the two Rakshas, I said: "I have no choice here.

Whatever this fair lady commands must be done. Take us both, therefore, to the place from which you brought her."

Bowing down in submission, they lifted us from the ground, carried us through the air, and placed us while it was yet night in the apartments of the princess. There she introduced me to her attendants, assigned me a room in the upper story where I might most easily escape detection, and appointed them to keep watch so that no one might enter her apartments without notice. I had thus abundant opportunities of being with the princess; but though my love daily increased, I made no further advances to her.

One day some of her women came with tears in their eyes, and bowing down to my feet, said, with whispering timid voice, "O gracious sir, our lady is doubly yours, since she was gained by your own valour when you rescued her from death, and is assigned to you by the all-powerful God of Love. Do not let her languish in vain. Make her your wife without delay." With this request I could not refuse to comply, and taking the hand of the princess, I declared our solemn union.

For a time we enjoyed the greatest happiness. It was destined, however, to be of no long duration; our separation was at hand, for now was the time of spring, when the trees were covered with blossoms bent down by the eager bees, and the song of birds was resounding among their branches waved by the soft south wind, bearing perfume from the sandal groves of Malaya; at which season the king was accustomed to go with all his court to the sea-shore, and there, in tents under the shade of lofty trees, to enjoy the cool sea breezes.

My bride of course went with the rest; and as there was no possibility of concealing me in such a place, I was obliged, though reluctantly, to let her depart alone, consoling myself by looking forward to her return.

The royal party had not long been gone, when news was brought to the city that the king and all his court, thinking only of enjoyment, and unsuspicious of danger, had been captured by Jayasinha, King of Andhra, who, sailing with a large fleet, had suddenly landed and taken them by surprise.

This news caused me the greatest consternation. "Jayasinha," I thought, "will certainly be captivated by the beauty of the princess; she will take poison rather than submit to his embraces; and I could not long survive her, for how could I live without her?"

While perplexed with this thought, and not knowing what to do, I heard of a brahman just arrived from Andhra, who was full of a strange event which had lately happened there.

"The King of Andhra," he said, "has long been a bitter enemy of the King of Kalinga, and having taken him prisoner, was about to kill him, but he has fallen in love with the princess Kanakalekha, and wishing to marry her, not only spares her father's life, but treats him with kindness for her sake.

"An unexpected obstacle to the accomplishment of his wishes has, however, arisen; the lady has suddenly become possessed by an evil spirit, whose rage is greatest whenever the king visits her.

"Anxious for her recovery, he has offered a large reward to any one who shall succeed in driving out the demon, but as yet no one has been able to effect her cure."

This information filled me with hope, for I was well aware of the nature of the princess's disease, and knew that no one but myself could cure it. I was able, therefore, to form a plan for her deliverance, and quickly decided on the disguise to be adopted. At the time when I killed the magician, I had taken off his scalp, with all the mass of tangled hair, and had hid it in a hollow tree. I now went to the place, and taking out this scalp, fitted it on my own head; then rubbing over my whole body with dirt and charcoal dust, and dressing myself in old rags, I was completely disguised as an ascetic—and when I went into the neighbouring villages I was regarded as a very holy devotee, and had many applications from persons wishing for advice or seeking to be cured of diseases. This belief I encouraged to the utmost, and took care to keep up my credit by means of various tricks and contrivances.

In this manner I was soon able to collect a number of disciples, glad to live in idleness on the offerings continually brought to me, fully believing in my sanctity, entirely devoted to me, and ready to obey all my commands.

Having got together this troop of followers, I went to the side of a tank or small lake not far from the city of Andhra, built myself a hut, and made known that I intended to stay there for a time.

The news of my arrival was soon spread abroad by my disciples, who were loud in their praises of my miraculous powers, and the wonderful cures which I had effected; and great numbers of people came from the city to see me, either from curiosity or from the hope of receiving some benefit.

In a very short time wonderful stories about me were brought to the Raja. "There is now a very holy devotee sleeping on the ground near the lake; he is possessed of the most marvellous knowledge. There is no question which he cannot answer, no difficulty which he cannot solve. His power of healing is beyond belief; a few grains of dust fallen from his feet, when sprinkled on the head of the sick, are more efficacious than any medicine; and water in which his feet have been washed has cured in a moment diseases, and driven out evil spirits which have resisted for a long time all the efforts of physicians and exorcists.

Yet with all this he is exceedingly kind and condescending, and free from pride."

The king, hearing all this, thought: "This is just the person I am in need of; no doubt he will be able to cure the princess." He therefore determined to apply to me; but so great was his respect for my dignity and supernatural powers, that he did not venture to send for me, but came several times to see me, distributing each time money among my followers, before mentioning his request that I would drive out the evil spirit from the princess.

After hearing his statement, I looked very grave, and appeared for some time to be wrapped in profound meditation. At last I said: "Sir, you have done very right to apply to me; I will undertake that the lady shall be cured, but it would be useless for me to see her at present. The case is a very peculiar one, and the cure requires much thought and consideration; wait therefore for three days, then come again, and I will tell you what is to be done." On receiving this answer, the king went away very well satisfied.

That night, as soon as it was dark, telling my followers on no account to disturb me, I went, as if for private meditation, to one side of the tank, at some distance from the steps, and there dug a large hole in the bank sloping upwards, with the opening partly under water and concealed by loose stones above; taking care to throw the excavated earth into the tank.

On the third day, at dawn, I rearranged my dress as before, and having worshipped the all-seeing sun as he rose, returned to my followers.

I had not long been settled in my usual place when the king made his appearance, and bowing down to my feet, he awaited my pleasure.

Having kept him a short time in suspense, I thus addressed him: "Success does not come to the careless, but all advantages are attainable by the energetic; being devoted to your service, I have given my whole mind to the consideration of this difficult affair, and can now point out a certain way to success.

"The evil spirit by whom the princess is possessed cannot bear the sight of you in your present form, and therefore breaks out into fury when you appear. If your body can be changed, he will no longer be offended, and will immediately depart; there is no other way by which he can be driven out. I have therefore so prepared this lake that if you bathe in it in accordance with my directions, you will acquire a new and beautiful body acceptable to the lady, and she will no more be troubled with the evil spirit.

"You must therefore come here at midnight, and having stripped entirely, swim out into the middle of the tank, and there float on your back as long as possible. Presently a rushing noise will be heard, and the water will be troubled, and dash against the bank. As soon as the commotion has subsided, come forth; you will find that your body has become younger, stronger, and improved in every respect; and when you return to the palace there will be no further difficulty or obstacle on the part of the princess, who will immediately undergo a change in her feelings, and will long for your society as much as she now abhors it. All this is quite certain; you need not have the smallest doubt; but if you think proper, before deciding, consult your ministers, and be guided by their advice. If they consent, first worship the gods and propitiate them with offerings, make large donations to the brahmans and the poor, and come here to-night at the appointed time. That there may be no danger from alligators or concealed enemies, let the tank be thoroughly dragged with nets by a hundred fishermen, and place a line of soldiers all round it with torches in their hands a few steps from the water; with these precautions no possible harm can happen to you."

The enamoured king, very anxious for the expulsion of the supposed demon, and fully believing that I had the power to perform what I had promised, went away well pleased, and immediately consulted his ministers. They seeing how eager he was, and not anticipating any possibility of danger, readily approved of the proceeding.

Having obtained their consent the king returned to me, and finding that I was about to depart, earnestly entreated me to stay, saying that half the pleasure of success would be taken away if I were not there to witness it; but I answered that there were urgent reasons for my immediate departure, and that I had already remained longer than I had intended to do, solely on his account. I assured him that I had so prepared everything that my presence was now quite unnecessary, that I was about to disappear from the world, and that he would see me no more. Finding me quite determined, he took leave of me with many expressions of respect, and went back to his palace to give orders for the performance of all that I had directed.

Accordingly, a large number of fishermen with nets were engaged, by whom the lake was thoroughly dragged, and large donations were made to the brahmans and the poor. Towards evening, soldiers with torches were placed all round the tank, and at midnight the king, attended by a numerous retinue, and followed by a great crowd anxious to witness the expected miracle, came to the steps leading down to the water, and having undressed there in a tent which had been pitched for that purpose, plunged in and swam out to the middle.

Meanwhile I had said to my followers: "I

have no further need of you; I am about to retire to a lonely place to practise meditation; you may now leave me; go, and my blessing be upon you." Well satisfied with the gifts they had received, they departed; and when they were gone I slipped unobserved into the lake, and entered the hole which I had prepared. There I remained till I heard the noise of the crowd who came with the king, and perceived him floating on the surface. Diving cautiously under him, I pulled him down, strangled him, and dragged the body into the hole; then swimming to the steps, I boldly came forth, to the astonishment of the attendants, who, though they had expected a miracle, were scarcely prepared for such a great change. No one, however, doubted that I was really their sovereign, and having dressed and mounted an elephant, I entered the city, escorted by the soldiers and followed by a great crowd of people, who had come forth from curiosity, and were loud in their praises of the pious man who had wrought such a miracle.

That night I was unable to sleep. In the morning I summoned all the ministers and counsellors, and said: "Behold the power of piety and penance. That holy man has performed a great miracle, and bestowed on me this new body, which you see, by means of the tank which he has consecrated, and through the favour of the gods, whom he had long propitiated; after such a manifestation, who shall doubt their power? Let the faces of all unbelievers be bowed down by shame; let a great and solemn festival be made with song and dance in honour of Brahma, Siva,

Yama, and the other deities, the rulers of the world, and distribute much money among the poor."

This speech was received with great approbation, and all, congratulating me and praising the gods, performed the duties imposed upon them.

After this I went to the women's apartments, and there the first person whom I met was a very devoted servant of the princess, who had been especially attentive to me. She, not imagining what had occurred, would have let me pass without especial notice; but I called her, and said: "Have you never seen me before?"

Then indeed she opened her eyes wide with joy and astonishment, saying: "Can it be possible? is not this a delusion? Tell me what it all means."

I gave her a brief account of what had happened, and sent her to prepare my wife. How glad she was to see me you may well imagine.

So well did we manage, that the secret was kept, no suspicion even arose, and all the people were rejoiced at the favourable change, not only in the person, but in the temper and disposition of their sovereign.

In due time I was publicly married to the princess, and reinstated her father in his kingdom.

I have now come here with an army to assist the King of Anga, and have thus obtained the great happiness of seeing you again.

The prince, having heard this story, said: "Your cleverness has indeed been great, and your personation of the Siddha wonderful.

May you long continue to possess such wisdom and prudence, combined with wit and cheerfulness." Then, looking at Visruta, he said: "It is now your turn;" and he forthwith began:—

ADVENTURES OF VISRUTA.

MY LORD, as I was wandering one day in the forest of Vindhya, I met with a very handsome boy, standing by the side of a well, crying bitterly. When I asked what was the matter, he said: "The old man who was with me, when trying to get water from this well, fell in, and I am unable to help him. What will become of me?"

Hearing this, I looked down the well, which was not very deep, and saw the old man standing at the bottom, the water not being sufficient to cover him. By means of a long and tough stem of a creeper, I pulled him up safely; then using it again as a rope, with a cup made from the hollow stem of a bamboo, I drew water for the poor child, who was half dead with thirst; and finding that he was suffering from hunger also, I knocked down some nuts from the top of a high tree with a well-aimed blow of a stone.

The old man was very grateful for my timely assistance; and when we were all comfortably seated in the shade, he gave me, at my request, a long account of the circumstances which had brought him there, saying:—

"There was formerly a King of Vidarba remarkable for wisdom and justice, learned in the Scriptures, a protector of his subjects (by whom he was much beloved), a terror to his enemies, wise in political science, upright and honest in all his actions, kind to his dependents, grateful for even small services, and gracious to all. Having lived the full age of man, he died, leaving a prosperous kingdom to his son Anantavarma, a young man of great abilities, but caring more for the mechanical arts, music, and poetry, than for his duties as a ruler.

"One day, one of his father's old counsellors in private addressed him thus: 'Sire, your majesty, with the advantage of royal birth, has almost every good quality that can be desired; your intelligence is very great; your knowledge superior to that of others; but all this, without instruction in political science and attention to public affairs, is insufficient for a king; void of such knowledge, he is despised, not only by foreigners, but by his own subjects, who, disregarding all laws, human and divine, at last perish miserably, and drag down their sovereign in their fall. A king who has not political wisdom, however good his eyesight may be, is regarded by the wise as a blind man, unable to see things as they are. I entreat you, therefore, to give up the pursuits to which you are so devoted, and to study the art of government. Your power will then be strengthened, and you may long reign over a happy and prosperous people.'

"To this exhortation the young king appeared to listen attentively; and said: 'Such is the teaching of the wise; it ought to be followed.'

"After dismissing the old counsellor, the king went into the women's apartments, and began to talk to them of the exhortation which he had just received. His observations were attentively listened to by one of his constant attendants, who determined, if possible, to turn the king's thoughts in another direction, and prevent him from being influenced by the good advice which had been given. This man had many accomplishments; he was skilled in dancing, music, and singing; quick at repartee; a good story-teller; full of fun and jokes; but devoid of honour and honesty; false, slanderous, a receiver of bribes, a bad man in every way; yet, from his wit and humour, very acceptable to the king, whom he now thus addressed: 'Wherever there is a person of exalted position, there are always clever rogues ready to prey upon him, and, while degrading him, to accomplish their own base purposes. Some, under the guise of religion, will tell him: "The happiness of this world is shortlived and fleeting; eternal happiness can only be obtained by prayer and penance;" and so they persuade him to shave his head, wear a dress of skins, gird himself with a rope of sacred grass, and, renouncing all pleasures and luxuries, to betake himself to fasting and penance, and give away his riches to the poor, meaning, of course, themselves; some of these religious impostors will even persuade their dupes to renounce children, wife—nay, even life itself.

"'But suppose a man to have too much sense to be deluded in this way, they will try a different plan; to one they will say: "We can make gold; only furnish us with the means, and your riches shall be increased a thousandfold;" to another: "We can show you how to destroy all your enemies without a weapon;" to another: "Follow our advice, and, though you are nobody now, you shall soon become a great man."

"'If their victim is a sovereign, they will

say to him: "Four branches of study are said to be proper for kings—the vedas, the purānas, metaphysics, and political science; but the first three are of very little advantage; they may safely be neglected, and he should give up his mind to the last only. Are there not the six thousand verses composed for the use of kings, and containing the whole science? Learn these by heart, and you will be prepared for all emergencies." So then he must set to work to learn all these crabbed rules. He must, according to them, distrust every one, even wife or son. He must rise early, take a very scanty meal, and immediately proceed to business.

"'First he must go over accounts, and balance income and expenditure; and while his rascally ministers pretend to have everything very exact, they have forty thousand ways of cheating him, and take good care of themselves.

"'Then he must sit in public, and be tired to death with receiving frivolous complaints and petitions, and will not even have the satisfaction of doing justice; for, whether a cause be just or not, his ministers will take care that the decision shall be according to their own interests.

"'Then he is allowed a short time for bathing, dressing, and dining; if, indeed, the poor wretch can venture to dine, with the constant fear of poison in his mind.

"'After this he must remain a long time in council with his ministers, perplexed with their conflicting arguments, and unable to understand even the half of them; while they, pretending to act impartially, get everything settled as they had previously agreed and by twisting and distorting the reports of spies and emissaries, manage to serve themselves and their friends, and to get credit for putting down disturbances which they themselves had excited.

"'He is now allowed to take a little amusement, but the time for this is restricted to an hour and a half.

"'Then he must review his army; hear the reports of the commander of his forces; give orders for peace or war; and act upon the accounts brought by spies and emissaries.

"'However weary he may be with all this, he must sit down and read diligently, like some poor student, for several hours. Then at last he may retire to rest; but before he has had half enough sleep, he will be awaked in the early morning; and the priests will come to him, and say: "There is an unfavourable conjunction of the planets; evil omens have appeared; there is danger impending; the gods must be propitiated; let a great sacrifice be made to-day. The brahmans are continually engaged in supplicating the gods on your behalf; your prosperity is dependent on their prayers; they are miserably poor, and have many children to support; let large donations be made." Thus the greedy wretches, under the pretence of religion, are continually robbing the king and enriching themselves.

"'This is the sort of life which you will have to lead, if you give yourself up to the guidance of those greybeards; and, after all, though you may have studied and studied, pored over their musty volumes, and listened to their tedious lectures, you are not sure of doing right.

"'And who are these fellows who set themselves up for wise men? Do they always do right? Are they not often themselves cheated by the unlearned? Common sense is far better than all this learning; instinct and feeling will guide us in the right way; even an infant without teaching finds out how to draw nourishment from the mother's breast. Cast aside, then, the rules and restrictions with which these old fools would bind you. Follow your natural inclinations, and enjoy life while you can. You possess youth, beauty, and strength. You have a large army, ten thousand elephants, and three hundred thousand horses; your treasury is full of gold and jewels, and would not be emptied in a thousand years. What more would you have? Life is short, and those who are always thinking of adding to their possessions, go on toiling to the last, and never really enjoy them.

"'But why should I waste your time with needless arguments? I see you are already convinced. Commit, then, the cares of government to your ministers; spend your time with your ladies, and congenial friends like me; enjoy drinking, music, and dancing, and trouble yourself no more with affairs of state.'

"Having thus spoken, he prostrated himself in very humble attitude at the feet of his master, who remained for a time silent, as if undecided.

"The women, who had been listening with delight to all that was said, seeing his hesitation, assembled round him, and, with sweet words and caresses, easily persuaded him to follow his own inclination and theirs.

"From that time the young king, given up entirely to pleasures and amusements, left the affairs of the kingdom to his ministers; and, while allowing them to manage as they pleased, provided they did not trouble him, openly treated them with insolence and neglect, and even took pleasure in hearing them ridiculed by the worthless parasites who surrounded him, so that even the wisest of his ministers, while lamenting the sad state of affairs, could only acknowledge their inability to remedy it, and wait till some great public calamity, or the invasion of the country by a neighbouring sovereign, who was gradually extending his dominions by force or cunning, should bring the young king to his senses.

"Ere long, what they had expected came to pass; for the King of Asmaka, who had for some time coveted the country, but did not dare openly to invade it while it was strong and prosperous, took measures in secret to weaken the authority of Anantavarma, and diminish his resources; and, lest he should perchance see the error of his ways and abandon his vicious courses, he secretly gave a commission to the son of one of his ministers, a young man of great abilities and agreeable manners, an eloquent flatterer and amusing companion, who arrived at the court of Anantavarma, attended by a numerous retinue, as if travelling about for his own pleasure.

"This man soon became intimate with the king, and took care to fall in with all his tastes, and to justify and praise every pursuit which he engaged in.

"Thus, if he saw the king fond of hunting, he would say: 'What a fine manly sport this is! How it strengthens the body, braces the spirits, and quickens the intelligence! While roaming over hill and dale, you become acquainted with the country; by destroying the deer and wild buffaloes, you benefit the husbandmen; by killing the tigers and other wild beasts, you make travelling safer.' And he would go on in this way, without any allusion to the damage and destruction caused by the king's hunting expeditions.

"If gambling was the favourite amusement, or there was excessive devotion to women, or to drinking, he would very ingeniously bring forward everything that could be said in favour of them, passing over their disadvantages in silence. If the king was lavish to his dependants, he would praise his generosity; if cruel, he would say: 'Such severity is good; you maintain your own dignity by it; a king ought not to be like a patient devotee, submitting to insults, and ready to forgive.'

"In this manner that wicked wretch obtained great influence over the king, and employed it to lead him into all sorts of excesses.

"With such an example before them, all classes gradually became corrupted. The magistrates neglected their duties, and thought only how they might enrich themselves; great criminals, who could bribe, escaped with impunity; the weak were oppressed by the strong; violence and robbery were rampant; disturbances broke out on all sides; and severe and indiscriminating punishments only stirred up indignation, without repressing crime. The revenue diminished, while expenditure was increasing; everywhere loud complaints were heard, and great distress prevailed.

"As if all this were not sufficient, the cruel King of Asmaka sent emissaries in all directions to mix unsuspectedly with the inhabitants of Vidarba, and do as much mischief as possible.

"Some would distribute subtle poisons in various ways; some would stir up quarrels between neighbouring villages, and so cause party fights; some contrived to let loose a furious elephant into a crowd, or get up an alarm by other means, and so cause a sudden panic, in which the people trampled down each other, and many lives were lost; others, disguised as hunters, promising abundance of game, would tempt men into some narrow valley, between high mountains, where they were devoured by tigers, or, unable to find their way out again, perished of hunger and thirst.

"By these and many other devices, they succeeded in destroying life and weakening the country, so that less resistance might be offered to the invader.

"Then, thinking the time to be arrived, the King of Asmaka prepared for war. Meanwhile, his emissary was leading on the foolish young king to destruction; and at this very time, as if in perfect security, he was amusing himself with the performances of a celebrated actress and dancer, having, at the instigation of his treacherous friend, persuaded her, by large donations, to leave the King of Kuntala, with whom she was a great favourite.

"Indignant at such an insult, that king was easily persuaded to join the King of

Asmaka, who had already obtained several other allies eager to have a share in the expected conquest and plunder.

"Thus, when the country was actually invaded, no effectual resistance was made; Anantavarma was easily defeated, and fell into the power of his cruel enemy.

"The cunning King of Asmaka, who had gained his allies by many liberal promises, had no intention of sharing the conquered country with any one; he professed, however, great disinterestedness; declared that he should be contented with a very small part; and, having desired his allies to arrange between themselves what each should take, contrived, by his intrigues, to make them quarrel over the division. The result was that they fought with, and so weakened each other, that he was able to disregard their claims, and to annex the whole of the conquered country to his own dominions.

"After the defeat and death of Anantavarma, an old and faithful minister escaped with the queen and her two children, this boy and his elder sister Manjuvādini, together with a few faithful followers, including myself; and though the old minister was taken ill and died on the road, the rest arrived safely at Mahishmati, where the queen was well received by the king Amittravarma, a half-brother of her husband, and where she devoted herself to the education of her son, hoping that he might one day recover his father's kingdom.

"After a time, however, that king sought to marry his brother's widow; and, having been rejected by her, determined to take revenge by killing her son.

"The queen, having discovered his intentions, sent for me, and said: 'My life is wrapped up in this boy; I can endure anything, so long as he is safe; take him and make your escape at once; I know not where to send you, but if you can find a safe refuge, let me know, and I will come to you, if possible.'

"In obedience to her commands, I took the boy, succeeded in escaping with him, and reached a shepherd's hut on the borders of this forest. There we stayed a few days till I saw a man whom I suspected to be searching for us. Fearing discovery, I left the cottage, and entered the forest. Here, while trying to get water to quench the poor child's burning thirst, I slipped into the well, where I should have perished but for your timely assistance; and now, having done us this kindness, will you add to it by protecting the boy, and helping us to reach a place of safety?"

"Who was his mother?" I asked. "Of what family was she?"

"She is the daughter of the King of Oude," he answered, "and her mother was Sagaradatta, daughter of Vaisravana, a merchant of Pātāliputra."

"If so," I replied, "she and my father are cousins by the mother's side; this boy is therefore my relation, and has a right to my protection."

The old man was much pleased at hearing this, and I promised not only to protect the boy, but to contrive some means for reinstating him in his proper position, and overcoming that wicked King of Asmaka with cunning equal to his own.

For the present, however, the most needful

thing was to procure food. While I was considering how to obtain this, two deer passed, pursued by a forester, who shot three arrows and missed them, and, in despair, let fall his bow and two remaining arrows. Hastily snatching up these, I discharged the arrows in rapid succession, and killed both the deer; one of them I gave to the hunter, the other I prepared, and roasted a part of it for ourselves.

The forester was astonished by my skill, and delighted at the acquisition of so much food; and it occurred to me that I might get some information from him. I asked him therefore: "Do you know anything of what is going on at Mahishmati?"

"I was there early this morning," he answered, "for I had a tiger skin and other skins to sell, and great festivities were in preparation; the Prince Prachandavarma, the king's younger brother, is about to marry the Princess Manjuvādini, and the rejoicings are on this account."

After the forester was gone, I said to the old man (whose name was Nālijangha): "That wretch Amittravarma is trying to make it up with his sister-in-law by promoting a good marriage for her daughter; no doubt he thinks to persuade her to recall her son, that he may have him in his power. Do you therefore leave the boy with me, and go back at once to his mother. Tell her how you have met with me, and that the child is quite safe under my protection; but give out in public that he has been carried off and devoured by a tiger. I shall come to the city disguised as a beggar; do you wait for me near the cemetery."

All this he promised to do, and set off

immediately, having first received further directions for the guidance of the queen.

After some days, it was generally understood at Mahishmati that the boy who had escaped into the forest had been killed by a tiger; and the king, secretly rejoicing, went to condole with the mother. She appeared as if greatly distressed by the news, and said to him: "I look upon the death of my son as a judgment upon me for not complying with your wishes, and am therefore now ready to become your wife."

The old wretch was delighted at her compliance, and preparations were made for the marriage.

On the appointed day, in the presence of a numerous assembly, she took a small leafy branch, and dipping it in what appeared to be water, but which really contained a deadly poison, struck him gently with it on the face, saying: "If you are acting right, this will not injure you; if you are sinning in taking me, your brother's wife, and I am faithful to my husband, may this be like the blow of a sword to you."

Such was the strength of the poison that he fell dead almost instantaneously. Then dipping the same branch into other water containing an antidote, she struck her daughter in a similar manner; and, as no injury followed, the spectators were fully convinced that the death of Amittravarma was a punishment from heaven.

Soon after this (by my directions, and in order to throw him off his guard), she said to Prachandavarma: "The throne is now vacant; you should occupy it at once, and make my daughter your queen."

He listened to the suggestion; and, as the young boy, the nephew of the late king, was supposed to be dead, no opposition was made by the people.

Then the Queen Vasundhara (also by my directions) sent for some of the late king's ministers, and of the elders of the city, whom she knew to be ill-affected towards Prachandavarma, and said to them: "Last night the goddess Durga appeared to me in a vision, and said: 'Your child is safe; I myself, in the form of a tigress, carried him away, to save him from his enemies. In four days from this time Prachandavarma will suddenly die; on the fifth day let all the authorities assemble round my temple on the bank of the river, and close the doors, after having ascertained that no one is concealed inside. After waiting one hour, the door will open and a young brahman will come forth, holding your son by the hand. That boy will become King of Vidarba, and that brahman is to marry your daughter.' "

After the divine manifestation in favour of the queen when Amittravarma was struck dead, this account of the vision was readily believed by her hearers, who promised to keep the secret and to be guided by her directions.

When the fourth day arrived I entered the city, disguised as a beggar, and brought the boy to his delighted mother, who introduced me to her daughter, whom I greatly admired, and she, though agitated, was evidently pleased with me, even under such a disguise.

I did not venture to stay long, and after receiving an alms and assuring the queen that the imagined dream would prove true, I went away, taking the boy with me, and at parting, in order to deceive her attendants, she said aloud: "Your application shall not have been in vain; I will take care to protect your boy."

Nālijangha, the old servant whom I had rescued in the forest, met me on my arrival, and was waiting at the place which I had appointed. I went to him there and asked him for information as to the movements and occupations of the new king. "That doomed man," he answered, "thinking all obstacles removed, and rejoicing at his accession to power, is now amusing himself in the palace gardens, with a number of actors, tumblers, and dancing girls."

"I could not have a better opportunity," I replied; "do you therefore stay here with the boy, and wait for me in this old ruin. I shall not be long gone."

I then dressed myself in the clothes of a tumbler, which I had brought with me for the purpose, went boldly into the garden, presented myself to the king, and asked for permission to exhibit my skill before him. This was readily granted; an opportunity was soon given me of showing what I could do, and I obtained much applause from the spectators. After a time I begged some of those present to lend me their knives, and I caused much astonishment by the way in which I appeared to balance myself on the points. Then, still holding one of the knives, I imitated the pouncing of a hawk and an eagle, and having by degrees got near the king, I threw the knife with such good aim, that it pierced him to the heart, and I shouted out at the same time, "Long live Vasantabhãnu!" that it might be supposed I had been sent by him. After this, dashing by the guards, who tried to stop me, I suddenly leaped over the wall, and before any of my pursuers could cross it, I had run a long way on the other side. Doubling back, I got behind a great heap of bricks, and from thence, concealed by the trees, succeeded in reaching the ruins unobserved. Here I changed my clothes and went back to the city, as if nothing had happened.

In order to have everything ready for my intended concealment, I had gone secretly the day before to the Temple of Durga, and had there made an underground chamber, communicating with the interior through an opening in the wall, which was carefully closed with a large stone, and now, taking the boy with me, I entered the hiding place, having been furnished with suitable dresses and ornaments, sent by the queen, through Nālijangha.

The assassination of Prachandavarma was universally attributed to his enemy, the King of Asmaka, and the first part of the prophecy of Durga, as told by the queen, being thus accomplished, there was no doubt, on the part of those who were in the secret, as to the fulfilment of the remainder.

In the morning a great crowd was assembled round the temple; for although the secret of the queen's vision had been kept, it was generally understood that something wonderful was to take place there.

Presently the queen and her attendants arrived, entered the building, and paid their devotions to the goddess, after which the whole temple was carefully searched, to make sure that no one was concealed there, and all having withdrawn, the doors were closed, and the people stood without in silence, anxiously awaiting the pleasure of the goddess.

A band then began to play and the kettle-drums were loudly struck, so that the sound reached me in the hiding-place. At this, which was the preconcerted signal, I made a great effort, moved the large stone, and came forth with the boy into the temple. Having changed our dresses, I placed the old ones in the hole, carefully refitted the stone, and throwing the temple door wide open, stood in front of the astonished multitude, holding the young prince by the hand.

While they were gazing in bewilderment, I thus addressed them: "The great goddess Durga, who lately showed herself in a vision to the queen, has been pleased to restore to his longing mother this child, whom she, in the form of a tigress, had carried away, and she commands you, by my mouth, to accept him as your sovereign."

Then turning to the queen, I said :—"Receive your child from the hands of Durga, who will henceforth protect him as her own son; and by her command accept me as the husband of your daughter."

To the ministers and elders I said :—"The goddess has brought me here, not merely as a messenger of her will, but as a defender of your country from that wicked King of Asmaka, whose cruel and unscrupulous intrigues are well known; accept me, therefore, as your deliverer, and as the guardian of the young king appointed by Durga."

Upon this all broke out into loud acclamations, saying: "Great is the power of the glorious Durga! happy the country of which you are the protector!" and I was conducted in triumph to the palace, together with the queen, who could now openly show her joy at the recovery of her son.

So well had I managed, that no suspicion arose of the deception which had been practised, and all the people venerated the young king as being especially under the protection of the goddess, and me as the agent chosen by her for his restoration.

Thus my authority was well established. I caused, in due time, the young prince to be formally proclaimed king, and had him carefully educated; and I myself received the hand of the lovely Manjuvādini, as the reward of my services and in obedience to the commands of Durga.

After some time, however, I began to reflect: "Though my position now seems quite secure, yet, after all, I am a foreigner here, and when the first burst of admiration is over, people may perhaps begin to ask, 'Who is this stranger who has come among us in such a mysterious manner? and what is he that he should thus lord it over us?' And it occurred to me that if I could make friends with an old and much-respected minister, named Aryaketu, so as to trust him entirely, he might be of great assistance to me."

Before, however, making any overtures to him, I desired Nālijangha to try him secretly and ascertain his feelings towards me.

My agent, therefore, had many interviews with him, and tried to persuade him that it was not for the good of the country that a stranger and foreigner should occupy such an important position, which ought rather to be held by a native, and that it would be very desirable to get rid of me.

To all this Aryaketu answered: "Do not speak against so good a man, and one of such wonderful ability, endowed with such great courage, generosity, and kindness. So many good qualities are rarely found united in one person. I esteem the country very fortunate in having such a ruler, and am convinced, that through him the King of Asmaka will one day be driven out, and our prince established on his father's throne. Nothing shall induce me to plot against such a man."

After hearing this from Nālijangha, I tried the old minister in various ways, and seeing no reason to doubt his fidelity and attachment, I gave him my full confidence, and found him a most useful friend.

With his advice and assistance, I was able to appoint efficient officers in every department. I encouraged religion and punished heresy; I kept each of the four castes in their proper sphere, and without oppressing the people, I collected a large revenue, for there is nothing worse than weakness in a ruler, and without money he cannot be strong.

[Here the story breaks off abruptly.]

LITERAL TRANSLATIONS.

PAGE 244.

MY LORD, I, having a common cause with my friends of wandering, saw among the Suhmans, in the outer park of a city called Damalipta, a great festal crowd. There, in a bower of Atimukta creepers, I saw a certain young man amusing himself with the sound of a lute. I asked him: "Worthy sir, what is this festival called? on what account is this beginning? or through what cause do you stand in solitude, accompanied (only) by your lute, as if out of spirits, not having done honour to the festival?"

He replied: "The King of Suhma, called

Tungadhanwa, being without offspring, begged from the feet of Durga, called Vindhyavāsiní,* dwelling in this abode, having her love for the abode in Vindhya forgotten, two children, and by her in a vision to him sleeping near (her temple) direction was given: 'There shall be produced of thee one son, and one daughter shall be born; but he shall be in subjection to her husband. But let her, beginning from the seventh year till her marriage, propitiate me every month while the moon is in Krittika (the constellation of the Pleiades), with the ball-dance, for the obtaining an excellent husband; and whom she likes, to him she is to be given: and let this festival be called the Ball Festival.' So she said.

"Then in a very short time the beloved

* The inhabitant of Vindhya.

queen of the king, named Mediní, bore a son, and a daughter was born at the same time. That damsel, called Kandukavati, will to-day propitiate the goddess having the moon as a diadem.

"But her friend, Chandrasena by name, her foster-sister, was beloved of me; and in these days she has been violently besieged by the king's son Bhimadhanwa. Therefore I, distressed, perplexed at heart by the pain of the arrow-darts of Kama, somewhat consoling myself with the soft tones of the lute, occupy a solitary place."

And at that moment there came near a certain sound of anklets, and a certain lady came up. He indeed having seen her, with eyes opened wide, having risen up, having been embraced by her, sat down; and he said: "This is the (lady) dear as my life, separation from whom, burning as it were, burns me up; and by that prince the robber of this, my life, I am brought to a state of coldness, as if by death; and I shall not be able, saying he is the king's son, to practise loyalty towards him; therefore, having caused myself to be favourably regarded by her, I will abandon a life which has no remedy."

But she, with her face full of tears, said: "O beloved, do not, on my account, engage in violence. Thou, who having been born of a worthy merchant, Arthadāsa, wast called Kosadāsa by thy parents, art called by thy enemies Vèsadāsa (slave of a girl), from thy excessive attachment to me. Thou thyself being dead, I should imagine the popular saying would be (he was) Nrisansa-Vesa—the slave of a wicked one. But now take me to any place you will."

But he said to me: "Friend, in the regions seen by you, which was (the most) prosperous, abounding in corn, and having the greatest number of good men?"

To him, having laughed a little, I said: "Wide is this (world bounded by) ocean and sky. There is no end of pleasant regions in one place or another. But, indeed, if I should not be able to produce some plan causing you to live comfortably here, then, indeed, I will show you the way."

Meanwhile, the sounds of jewel-anklets arose. Now she, in a hurry, said: "My lord's daughter Kandukavati is come to propitiate Durga with playing at ball; and she is of unforbidden sight in this Kanduka (ball) festival. May the eye of you going to see her be successful; I must be keeping near her." So saying, she went away, and we two followed her.

I first saw the red-lipped (lady) standing on the floor of a jewelled stage; and she, seen by me a stranger and at a distance, immediately settled in my heart. And I, having my mind occupied by astonishment, thought: "Is this Lakshmi? for the lotus is not placed in her hand; but in her (Lakshmi's) hand there is a lotus, and she (the goddess) has been all enjoyed by Vishnu, and by former kings; but in this (lady) there is unimpaired faultless youth."

While I was thus reflecting, she, faultless in every limb, touching the ground with the tips of her stretched-out fingers, having her dark curled locks shaken, having with agitation saluted the mighty goddess, took hold of the ball, resembling (in colour) the god without a body (*i.e.* Kama) having his eye reddened by no slight passion; and having dropped it with graceful languor to the ground, having struck it, gently rising, with her bud-like hand having the delicate fingers stretched out, the thumb a little bent; having thrown it up with the back of the hand, she caught it observed with active grace, in the air as it fell like a bunch of flowers joined with a circle of bees; and she discharged it in middling slow and quick musical time, throwing it very gently; and at that moment she displayed a quick movement with her feet; and when it stopped, she caused it to rise up with numerous blows; and, contrarywise, she caused it to rest; and she made it rise up like a bird, striking it regularly with her left and right hands when it was come straight to her side, and having caught it fallen when it had risen to a very great height, she practised a song-step ; and having caused it to go up in various directions, she made it come back again. Thus sporting sweetly in various ways, accepting the words of praise loudly spoken at every moment by the people with their feelings interested come near to the stage, she stands turned towards me (who was) leaning on the shoulder of Kosadāsa, having just then confidence produced in me, with flushed cheek and wide expanded eye. Then she being caused to have a glancing look like that of Kandarpa when first descended to earth, corresponding therewith. having her gracefully-curved creeper* eyebrows sportively playing ; with the network of the rays of light of her lips oscillated by the waves of

* Resembling tendrils.

the wind of her breath, like twigs moved in sport, as if beating off the bees eager to catch the perfume of her lotus-face. In the circular whirlings of the ball (caused) by very rapid striking, entering, as it were, a flowery cage, through bashfulness at sight of me; in the Panchavindhu movement shaking off, as if through fear, the five arrows of Kama simultaneously falling (on her); in the Gomuttrika steps quivering like the brightness shown in the cloud imitating forked lightning; in the harmonious movements of her feet, having the time kept by the sound of the jewelled ornaments; with her lower lip suffused with the brightness of a furtive smile; with the mass of her locks put up again when fallen down; with her jewelled girdle-belt sounding by knocking together; with the brightness of her muslin dress, agitated as it rested on her gracefully prominent full hips; with the beautiful ball, struck by the quivering, bent, and extended arms; with the arms like a loop, turned downwards; with her graceful hair reaching to the end of the back, rolled round upwards; with the game continued (and) not neglected from her rapidity in putting up the fallen-down golden leaf of the ear-ring; with the ball whirled inwards and outwards by the feet and hands throwing it up repeatedly; with the necklace lost to sight through bending down and rising up; the pearls without separation in falling and rising; with the wind of the little branch (stuck) in (or behind) the ear engaged in drying up the paint of the cheek spoilt by the perspiration breaking forth; with one hand engaged in holding back on the surface of her bosom the falling muslin dress; sitting down and rising up, closing and opening her eyes, striking on the ground or in the air, with one ball or more than one, she showed various sorts of play worth looking at.

PAGE 36.

After that, a certain damsel, adorned with a quantity of ornaments, made of jewels, who had become the chief of the whole race of women in the world, attended by a numerous train of modest female friends, having the gait of a swan, having come up softly, having made an offering to the most excellent brahman of one jewel of the form (colour) of flame, being asked by him: "Who art thou?"

Sorrowfully, with a low murmuring voice,

very gently, in a submissive attitude, said: "O excellent brahman, I am the daughter of a chief of Asuras, Kālindi by name. My father, the ruler of this world, great in dignity, in a battle in which the immortals were removed to a distance, was made a guest of the city of Yama by Vishnu, impatient of his own valour. Me, immersed in an ocean of grief at separation from him, a certain compassionate perfected devotee told: 'Damsel, a certain mortal, bearing a divine body, having become thy new husband, shall rule over the whole of Patala.'"

PAGE 309.

Having propitiated with clasped hands, put together in the form of the red lotus, the mass of rays coloured by the red sandalwood body of the thousand-eyed elephant of the eastern quarter having a thousand flames, the witness of things (which ought) to be done and not to be done, the unique sea-monster leaping over the row of cloud-waves of the celestial ocean, the graceful actor dancing on the stage of the golden rock, the one lion the tearer of the scented elephant of nocturnal darkness, the jewel arranged at the top of the pearl necklace the canopy of the stars; I went to my own dwelling. And three days being gone, when the lord of day had a splendour of colour common to it with the red chalk side of the peak of the western mountain, and was looking like the orb of one bosom of the Goddess of Twilight, united with the body of Siva, under the name of atmosphere, for the disparagement of the daughter of the king of mountains; that king also having come, stood in humble attitude, having his diadem eclipsed by the rays from the nails of the feet of this person placed on the ground; and he was thus addressed:—

PROPER NAMES, ETC., OCCURRING IN THE TALES.

Alaka, a mountain inhabited by Kuvera and the Yakshas.

Ambālika, the daughter of Sinhavarma, wife of Mantragupta.

Amittravarma, King or Governor of Mahishmati.

Anantavarma, King of Vidarba.

Apahāravarma, son of Prahāravarma, and one of the nine companions of Rājahansa.

Apsaras, heavenly females, nearly corresponding with the houris of the Mahometans.

Arthapāla, son of Kāmapāla, one of the nine companions of Rājahansa.

Arthapati, a merchant at Champa, who wished to marry Kulapālika.

Aryaketu, a minister and friend of Visruta.

Asura, a general term for various supernatural beings not regarded as gods, but in general hostile to them, nearly the same as the jins or genii of the "Arabian Nights."

Avantisundari, daughter of Mānasāra, wife of Rājavāhana.

Balabhadra, a merchant, husband of Ratnavati.

Bālachandrika, wife of Pushpodbhava, and friend of Avantisundari.

Bandhupāla, a merchant, father of Balachandrika.

Betel and pawn, a mixture for chewing, frequently offered in politeness, as snuff with us.

Bheels, savages, wild tribes, robbers.

Bhimadhanwa, brother of Kandukavati.

Buddhist, a disciple of Buddha. Buddha was a Hindoo reformer, whose followers were once very numerous in India, but at the date of these stories had been much diminished in number, through the persecutions of the brahmans. They still, however, form a large part of the population of Ceylon, Thibet, China, and some other countries, though the comparatively pure religion of the founder has for the most part degenerated into gross idolatry and unmeaning ceremonies.

Chakravāka, name of a bird quoted for affection, as turtle-doves by us.

Chandāla, a pariah, outcast.

Chandrasena, foster-sister of the Princess Kandukavati.

Chātaka, a bird supposed to be very fond of rain, and to make a loud noise at its approach.

Dhanamittra, husband of Kulapālika, friend of Apahāravarma.

Dharmapāla, one of Rājahansa's ministers.

Dharmavardhana, King of Sravasti.

Durga or *Kāli*, wife of Siva, a terrific goddess, delighting in human sacrifices.

Gaurí, wife of Siva.

Ghee, liquid butter, or butter which has been liquefied.

Indra, the chief of the inferior gods, presiding over the clouds, rain, thunder, &c.

Kailāsa, a mountain, part of the Himālaya chain.

Kalahakantaka, the man who fell in love with a portrait.

Kalindi, Queen of Pātāla, wife of Matanga.

Kalpasundari, wife of Vikatavarma, afterwards of Upahāravarma.

Kāma or *Kandarpa*, the God of Love.

Kāmamanjari, the actress who seduced the Muni.

Kāmapāla, son of Dharmapāla, minister and son-in-law of the King of Benares.

Kanakalekha, daughter of the King of Kalinga, wife of Mantragupta.

Kandukavati, the princess who performed the ball-dance.

Kantaka, the gaoler killed by Upahāravarma.

Kantimati, the wife of Kāmapala, mother of Arthapāla.

Kirāta, a savage, forester, Bheel.

Kosadāsa, lover of Chandrasena.

Kusa-grass, a scented grass, much used at sacrifices for laying offerings on, &c.

Kuvera, the God of Wealth, whose attendants were the Yakshas.

Magadha, the kingdom of Rājahansa.

Mahākāla, a famous temple of Siva, the object of many pilgrimages.

Mahishmati, name of a city.

Malaya, a mountain, or range of mountains, having many sandal trees, the perfume from which was supposed to be carried a long distance by the wind.

Mālwa, the kingdom of Mānasāra.

Mānāpala, the officer who guarded Vāmalochana.

Mānasāra, King of Mālwa, conqueror of Rājahansa.

Manibhadra, a Yaksha, father of Tārāvali.

Manjuvādini, daughter of Anantavarma, wife of Visruta.

Mantra, a verse or chapter in the vedas, any prayer or words recited as a charm.

Mārichi, a great muni seduced by Kāmamanjari.

Matanga, a brahman who went down to Pātāla together with Rājavāhana.

Mithila, a city or country, called also Videha.

Mitragupta, one of the nine companions of Rājavāhana.

Muni, a holy man devoted to study, meditation, and penance.

Nalijangha, the old man whom Visruta rescued from the well.

Nārāyana, a name of Vishnu, an incarnation of the three principal gods, Brahma, Vishnu, Siva.

Navamālika, daughter of the King of Sravasti, wife of Pramati.

Padmodbhava, one of Rājahansa's ministers.

Pātāla, a fabulous subterranean country.

Prachandavarma, King or Governor of Mahishmati, killed by Visruta.

Prahāravarma, King of Mithila, father of Apaharāvarma and Upahāravarma.

Priyamvada, Queen of Prahāravarma.

Purnabhadra, the reformed robber, servant of Kāmapāla.

Pushpapuri, the capital of Magadha.

Rāgamanjari, an actress, sister of Kāmamanjari.

Rājahansa, king of Magadha, father of Rājavāhana, the hero of the story.

Rakshas or *Rakshasas*, evil spirits or ogres, hostile to men, whom they used to devour.

Rati, a goddess, wife of Kāma.

Rishi, nearly the same as Muni, a holy man retired from the world, devoted to prayer and meditation.

Satyavarma, son of a minister of Rājahansa, and father of Somadatta.

Savara, fem. *Savari*, a savage, not a Hindoo.

Siddha (literally perfected), a very holy devotee.

Simanta, a religious ceremony performed on behalf of a woman at a certain period of pregnancy.

Sinhaghosha, the deposed King of Benares.

Sinhavarma, King of Anga, father of Ambālika.

Sitavarma, one of Rājahansa's ministers.

Sringālika, the nurse of Rāgamanjari.

Siva, one of the three chief gods or triad of the Hindoos, Brahma, Siva, and Vishnu, who are sometimes regarded as one, sometimes confounded with each other.

Sumantra, son of Dharmapāla.

Susruta, son of Padmodbhava.

Tārāvali, a Yaksha lady, wife of Kāmapala.

Vāmadeva, a holy man consulted by Rājahansa.

Vāmalochana, daughter of Viraketu, wife of Somadatta.

Vasumati, Queen of Rājahansa.

Vasundhara, Queen of Anantavarma the King of Vidarba.

Vidarba, name of a country.

Videha, a country called also Mithila.

Vidyādhara, one of the numerous demigods.

Vidyeswara, the conjuror who married Rājavāhana to Avantisundari.

Vikatavarma, King of Mithila, husband of Kalpasundari.

Vimardaka, a keeper of a gaming house, employed by Apahāravarma.

Viraketu, King of Pātali, father of Vāmalochana.

Yaksha, a sort of demigod or fairy, a servant of Kuvera.

Yama, God and Judge of the Infernal Regions.

Yati, an ascetic, a devotee.

Yavana, a Greek, an Arabian—any foreigner.

THE END.